Yorkshire's Secret Castles

Yorkshire's
Secret Castles

A Concise Guide and Companion

Paul C. Levitt

PEN & SWORD
HISTORY

First published in Great Britain in 2017 by
PEN AND SWORD HISTORY
an imprint of
Pen and Sword Books Ltd
47 Church Street
Barnsley
South Yorkshire S70 2AS

Copyright © Paul C. Levitt, 2017

ISBN 978 1 52670 620 1

Printed and bound in England
by CPI Group (UK) Ltd, Croydon, CR0 4YY

Typeset in Times New Roman by
CHIC GRAPHICS

Pen & Sword Books Ltd incorporates the imprints of Pen & Sword
Airworld, Archaeology, Atlas, Aviation, Battleground, Discovery,
Family History, Fiction, History, Maritime, Military, Military Classics,
Politics, Select, Social History, True Crime, Frontline Books, Leo
Cooper, Remember When, Seaforth Publishing, The Praetorian Press,
Wharncliffe Local History, Wharncliffe Transport. Wharncliffe True
Crime and White Owl.

For a complete list of Pen and Sword titles please contact
Pen and Sword Books Limited
47 Church Street, Barnsley, South Yorkshire, S70 2AS, England
E-mail: enquiries@pen-and-sword.co.uk
Website: www.pen-and-sword.co.uk

Contents

The earthworks in this book are listed alphabetically and there is no recommended viewing order. These sites are not a complete picture of all early Norman timber castles in Yorkshire.

Preface

Mention the word 'castle' and most people will immediately think of some idyllic old pile that attracts thousands of visitors in summer. But long before works in masonry were developed, castles were simply built from earth and timber. Some were abandoned when stone castles were built nearby and some were themselves upgraded in stone. Thrown up soon after the Norman Conquest nine-and-a-half centuries ago, these earth and timber castles are 'secret' in the sense that they have been largely forgotten, neglected, concealed or encroached upon by later developments. In a few cases they were engulfed, buried and even destroyed. Their existence and location remains obscure because at best there is little to see. But dig deeper and they all have a story to tell. Who built them and when? What did they look like originally? What traces remain and where can they be found? More than a century ago, antiquary W.M. I'Anson surveyed many of North Yorkshire's 'secret' castles. This book follows in his footsteps and uncovers much of the interesting information he collected on sites that have been largely undisturbed for centuries. It incorporates not only the 34 castles surveyed by I'Anson but also adds a further 41 sites that give a broader picture for the county of Yorkshire as a whole.

Acknowledgements

The author wishes to express his immense gratitude to the Yorkshire Archaeological & Historical Society in whose journal work by the late W.M. I'Anson F.S.A. was published more than 100 years ago and which was the inspiration for this book.

With a few exceptions, quotations throughout this work were obtained from the *Yorkshire Archaeological Journal*, Vol. 22, 303–399, 'The Castles of the North Riding', and Vol. 24, 258–262, 'Skipsea Castle'; they are republished with kind permission of the Yorkshire Archaeological & Historical Society.

W.M. I'Anson.

Chris I'Anson, a distant relative, and Bootham School in York kindly gave their kind permission to reproduce the only photos of W.M. I'Anson obtainable. Born on Boxing Day in 1871 at Saltburn-by-the-Sea on the North Yorkshire coast, William Mangles I'Anson attended Bootham School, York, where he won a prize in the Landscape Art category at the 1888 annual exhibition of York School Natural History, Literary and Polytechnic Society. I'Anson also wrote on historical subjects and his earliest work was published in Bootham School's *The Observer* – a series of collections of essays. In adulthood, he followed in his father's footsteps when he succeeded him as engineer of Cleveland Water Works, Saltburn.

I'Anson pursued his strong interest in history as a member of the Society of Antiquaries and of the Earthworks Committee of the Congress of Archaeological Societies. In the North Riding alone, he visited and surveyed 34 motte and bailey castles. He was also a prominent member of the Ancient Monument Committee for Yorkshire and was perhaps the first authority on medieval military effigies.

W.M. I'Anson (back row, seventh from the right) at Bootham School, York in 1888.

Interestingly, he belonged to the same family as Frances I'Anson, immortalised in the song 'The Lass of Richmond Hill'. William Mangles I'Anson died on 5 March 1926 at the relatively young age of 54.

I am further indebted to my talented friend Andreas Renou, who studied at the Royal College of Art, London and has a passion for drawing, painting and design. He has recreated scenes from a time when Yorkshire's 'secret' castles dominated the landscape nine centuries ago and has drawn all the ground plans contained in this book.

My thanks also go to Dennis Bromage for his inspirational photograph of Whitestone Cliff and the distant Hood Hill. A full-time professional landscape photographer who lives close to the North York Moors, Dennis has a passion for the outdoors and has captured perfectly the solitude of this castle site, the whereabouts of which remained a mystery for many years.

A final word of thanks goes to my wife for her patience and unflinching support while visiting what must have seemed like mere mounds of earth. I like to think that she now sees them as ancient and precious remnants of Yorkshire's secret castles.

Introduction

When the Normans invaded England in 1066, they conquered a land that remained hostile to their presence for many years. Norman barons were given land for their services and loyalty to the new king, William, Duke of Normandy, but very few felt secure. One of their first actions was to throw up earth and timber castles from which they could safely watch over and protect their newly conquered lands. Although a novelty to the English, Edward the Confessor had allowed favourites of the Norman nobility to erect castles several decades before his death and the subsequent Norman invasion. In this context, the earliest recorded castle in England dates back to 1048 (*Anglo-Saxon Chronicle*). After the invasion, revolts and their suppression prompted the erection of a large number of castles, the majority being built between 1071 and 1145. About 100 had been erected by the time of the Domesday Book, a full 20 years after the invasion. Today, more than 700 castle mounds (mottes) have been identified in England and Wales according to the late antiquary W.M. I'Anson. William the Conqueror alone is reputed to have raised about 100 mottes and his son added a further 100. The first of William's castles was at Hastings, but he built castles in every major Saxon town as part of a strategic plan. Norman barons, on the other hand, built them to fortify their home bases (caputs) from which they ruled over their lands (fiefs). In periods when loyalties became blurred, barons used the situation to reinforce and expand their lands and power at the expense of their neighbours. So, castles were necessary for protection not only against an unruly if not hostile population but also aggression from peers during infighting. Eventually they became symbols of military and economic power.

Earth and timber castles gave adequate protection against surprise attack and were relatively easy to erect from materials that were almost always close at hand. The most common form of castle comprised a group of buildings offering living quarters (hall), a kitchen, stable, barn and chapel, all contained within a ditch (foss) and rampart formed by the spoil from the ditch topped by a wooden fence (palisade). The motte was an elevated mound of earth topped with a wooden tower and protected by its own ditch and inner palisade, and the bailey was a further protected area within the outer palisade. Some castles with a motte, such as at Carlton-in-Coverdale, consisted of just a shelter within a palisade on top of the motte. Ringworks (castles built without a motte) had a tall wooden gatehouse to give a height advantage against attackers.

Ease of construction meant even less powerful and less wealthy barons could afford the relatively low cost of an earth and timber castle. Records show that the mighty castle mound known as Baile Hill at York took just over a week to build by the Conqueror's men. But military warfare moved on after the invasion and new techniques and weapons rendered these types of castle obsolete. Despite their enormous practicality and effectiveness, their one huge inherent weakness was being vulnerable to attack by fire. A century after the conquest, castle building entered a new phase. Outer defences, including palisades and gatehouses, were replaced using stone at the earliest opportunity. Naturally, the speed of this process depended heavily on finances, a convenient supply of stone and royal consent. When Henry II acceded to the throne in 1154, some 88 years after the Norman invasion, very few – only Richmond, Scarborough and Tickhill – of some 30 of North Yorkshire's strongholds had any stone defences. At the accession of Richard I in 1189, some 35 years after Henry and 123 years after the invasion, only a further three had any stone defences to speak of: Bowes, Castleton and Pickering. The stonework at Pickering was limited to the inner bailey, but other buildings ranged within the outer defences were also gradually replaced using stone. In due course, the stone hall became the second line of defence and gave further protection if the bailey was successfully stormed. It eventually evolved into the keep of later stone castles.

As well as the strengthening of existing fortresses using stone, considerably larger stone castles were erected close to existing earthwork castles, not least because of the strategic vantage points they afforded. Reverend George Young was an author who recognised a pattern in the location of castles. 'The Roman forts are intimately connected with the ancient baronial castles, and in some instances, the latter seem to have been erected on the sites of the former. This was probably the case with the old castle of Mulgrave (Foss), placed on the long ridge between Eastrow beck and Sandsend beck, above a mile from the sea. This idea is favoured not only by its strong position, and apparent connexion with the chain of Roman posts to the south, but by its proximity to the British *strength (fort)* already noticed. The Romans disposed their forts, so as to command the forts of the natives, of which we have an instance in the relative situation of the camps and station at Cawthorn, and the British *strength* at Cropton. Besides, it is easy to perceive, on examining the fragments of this castle, that they are not the relics of the original structure, but one built out of its ruins,' he wrote in 1817.

Many of the castles that had their defences fortified in stone took years and considerable fortunes to complete, and Yorkshire has some fine examples that have survived to this day. The English Civil War left many stone castles in ruins, but substantial remains still exist at Bolton in Wensleydale (arguably the finest example of a quadrangular palace-fortress in England), Conisborough, Helmsley, Middleham, Pickering, Pontefract, Richmond (one of the finest examples of an eleventh-century castle in Europe), Scarborough, Tickhill, York and to a lesser extent at Sandal, despite it once having been one of the grandest castles in the realm.

Understandably, the first earthwork castles rebuilt in stone were all in the hands of the monarch and were symbolic of royal power. Discontented with their wooden strongholds, barons grasped the opportunity presented by Henry II's death to persuade the relatively weaker Richard to grant them permission to update their fortresses using stone. In Yorkshire, Middleham, Skelton, Mulgrave (Foss) and Helmsley were among the first converted. And although the importance of castles had waned considerably by the middle of the fourteenth century, the aristocracy developed their stately homes as palace-fortresses for a further century. But this was more for comfort and prestige than defensive purposes.

Before its development in stone, an earth and timber fortress existed at Helmsley.

This book goes in search of castles that represent the earliest feudal stamp of the Normans on the landscape of Yorkshire. It is by no means a full account of every single fortress built by the Normans in the county of Yorkshire. Indeed, not all have survived and some sites have doubtless been wiped clean of earthworks by land cultivation and development. This book looks at sites that will appeal to the visitor for a variety of reasons. Many of the sites are situated off the beaten track and command superb views of outstandingly beautiful countryside, such as those clustered around the North York Moors. Others are close to populated areas and some are even in public areas such as parks, and thus easily accessible. Well-documented sites that are firmly on the tourist agenda are only briefly referenced.

As mentioned, some of the castles were subsequently developed in stone and are therefore conspicuous by their survival and are no longer 'secret' in the strictest sense. But the majority are secluded enough to be largely overlooked by the casual visitor or passerby. In some instances, visible remains have long since blended into the local scenery, either due to natural decay and neglect, vandalism, or uncaring (or unwitting) civil-engineering works of past centuries. Some sites are on private property and need the permission of the owners to view them; 'hidden' from general view, they go largely unnoticed by all but the most informed visitor. Indeed, many locals are blissfully unaware of what once existed on their very doorstep. One local historical society wrote on its website: 'The monument has suffered as the result of a long period of neglect. This is due in the main to the lack of awareness of many of the inhabitants. Trees outlining the perimeter of the earthworks have grown through default. Some have fallen and torn out the banking with major damage to the earthworks. The trees hide the spectacular nature of the hard work of the inhabitants who created the monument with few tools and much hard labour. A further feature of the state of the earthworks was the large amount of garden waste and other rubbish, which had been tipped into the ditch where it is accessible to the public. English Heritage urged the village to take greater care of the earthworks.' Enough said!

In many cases, visitors will see no more than grassed-over mounds. If ever upgrading took place in brick or stone, the remains may have disappeared and it needs imagination to see beyond what remains visible today. After nearly a millennium of silting down, traces of former timber defences have long since decayed. Even stone is not safe from the ravages of time. At Skipsea (East Riding), for instance, where development in stone is known to have taken place, the few remaining stones would scarcely fill a wheelbarrow. One can be forgiven for wondering how many local buildings have profited from its dereliction. Materials are also recorded as having been salvaged, transported over considerable distances and reused for other building projects. Mount Ferrant (East Riding) is just one example where this has occurred.

Contemporary depictions, as on the Bayeux Tapestry, help us build a mental picture of earth being dug to create a ditch and then used to form the ramparts and the motte, which would have been flattened and shored up using wood to encase the perimeter embankment. A wooden tower would then have been erected, giving an even better view of the

An impression of the first fortress at Skipsea, one of the most interesting of the late eleventh-century castles of the East Riding.

surrounding countryside, especially for archers to enjoy a clear shot at any intruders. The steep-sided ditch, perhaps some 3m deep, together with the elevated rampart forming the sides of the motte, would have presented a substantial and no doubt slippery obstacle to any attacker. Together with the timber palisade, the obstacle to be scaled would have approached 8m or more in height.

Ramparts and ditches are the main features and often the only ones to have survived the centuries. These basic defences formed a ringwork and represent the simplest and earliest form of a castle. Sometimes a double ringwork was built for extra security. The entrance would have been protected by a massive timber gatehouse standing 8m or more in height, with access across the ditch and into the inner sanctuary of the castle achieved via a retractable wooden bridge. The inner sanctuary or courtyard could be as small as 40m in diameter or much larger, depending on the importance of the manorial lord and the needs of his household.

Mottes could vary in height from 5 to 20m or more (no less than 22m at Tickhill). The size of the motte determined the building area and thus governed the type of wooden structure erected on the summit.

This last line of defence might be as extensive as safe living quarters for the lord and his immediate family or simply a lookout tower for positioning archers. The main living accommodation would have been in buildings located in the bailey or courtyard, which would assume the most easily defended shape depending on what natural defences were available. A promontory formed by a cliff on the inside bend of a river, for example, might give rise to a triangular or kidney-shaped bailey that could be easily covered by archers deployed on the motte. But various shapes are encompassed, including square, oblong and irregular-shaped baileys. Numerous mottes have survived the centuries. Some of the more substantial ones were further developed by the addition of stone shell keeps, such as at Pickering. Those that have survived the forces of erosion demonstrate what impressive obstacles mottes presented to attackers below.

Finally, let us not forget the fact that some of these castles, notably the so-called robber dens erected during times of civil warfare, were the scourge of the local populace and bad news for anyone who ventured into their sphere of influence. 'That a number of these castles were an intolerable infliction is quite certain, and these quiet green mounds which mark their sites could, were they able to speak, tell us many horrible tales of the bestiality and vicious cruelty of their inmates,' wrote I'Anson.

On that sobering note, you are invited to set your imagination free and travel back in time to discover Yorkshire's secret castles.

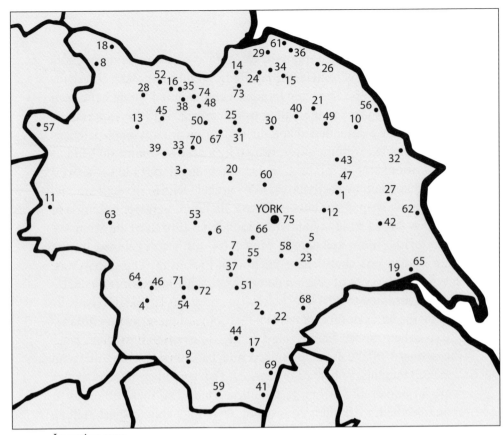

Location map.

ACKLAM

Acklam is a small village located roughly 6 miles due south of Malton and 14 miles northeast of York on the western slopes of the Yorkshire Wolds. It is surrounded by open farmland interspersed with woodland, with extensive views of the Vale of York from the Wolds escarpment to the east of the village. The area has been occupied since prehistoric times, as evidenced by finds from Bronze Age burials on nearby Acklam Wold. There are also Iron Age earthworks in the area and the land around it has been farmed for at least a thousand years. A Roman road that would have stretched from Brough (Petuaria) on the north bank of the Humber to Malton runs close to the village. And on the western edge of a ridge that rises above Acklam beck are the silted-down remains of a former motte and bailey fortress. Reminiscent of the Fossard fortress at Mount Ferrant in nearby Birdsall, but on a much smaller scale, the fortress at Acklam is thought to have been an outlying stronghold of the Fossard family or an earlier attempt at establishing a stronghold that was quickly abandoned.

The remains of a former motte and bailey fortress are on a ridge that rises above Acklam Beck.

1

Extensive views of the Vale of York unfold as you climb the Wolds escarpment to the east of Acklam.

As at Mount Ferrant, two ditches were dug across the steep-sided natural ridge and form the most visible features of the earthworks. The smallish motte, which stood at the highest point towards the western end of the east-to-west-running ridge would have originally been topped by a wooden tower and palisade. The northern scarp of the ridge still bears traces of a ditch and outer bank, both of which are still extant in the corner of a field to the immediate northwest of the castle. The gently sloping ground to the west of the motte would have served as a bailey. This was protected by the steeply scarped edge of the ridge. A ditch was dug across the ridge to protect the motte from the relatively level ground to the east, which would have formed a second bailey. The bailey was defended on its eastern side by an artificial scarp and ditch. A third bailey would have existed on the land between the eastern bailey and the modern road leading up Pasture Hill. This bailey would have extended to the modern field boundary. The site is visible from the road.

ADWICK-LE-STREET

Adwick-le-Street is a village in the Metropolitan Borough of Doncaster that lies just off the Great North Road (A1) and 4 miles north of Doncaster itself. To the southeast of the village, surrounded by arable farmland, is a recreational area of parkland known as Castle Hills where the earthworks of Hangthwaite Castle are located. The motte and bailey fortress is attributed to Nigel Fossard and originally belonged to the manor of Langthwaite, which was one of six manors Fossard held in 1086 as a subfeudary of the count of Mortain. It later became known as Hangthwaite, which commemorates a 'lost' village of which the faint earthworks can still be seen. Its former name, however, lives on in the name of a local lane, which leads past the site to a fortified manor house of a later date. The site is heavily overgrown, but the motte, ditches and counterscarp banks are still clearly defined. A kidney-shaped inner bailey can be traced to the north, as can a sub-rectangular outer bailey to the east. Between the motte and the inner bailey on the southwestern side the rampart ends in a small mound that hints at the existence of a barbican at some stage.

ALDBOROUGH

The village of Aldborough (now in North Yorkshire but historically part of the West Riding) is situated just to the southeast of Boroughbridge and not far from the Great North Road. It marks the site of the former Roman town of Isurium Brigantum, which was built at the strategic intersection of Hadrian's Wall and Dere Street – the Roman road leading from York to the Antonine Wall. Referred to in the Domesday Book as Burgh ('burh' meaning 'ancient fortification' in Old English), the prefix 'ald' (old) was added to the name by 1145 (Smith, 1961). Aldborough's importance declined when the River Ure crossing was moved to Boroughbridge during the Norman period. Nonetheless, a castle is recorded as having existed on a site to the south of the village known as Studforth Hill since 1158. Originally held by the Crown, it passed into baronial hands ('Stuteville' is one of several old names by which the site was known) but was retaken by the Crown in 1205 (Brown, 1959).

Listed in 2014 as a possible motte and bailey earthworks, the former castle site is different from what one would expect to see had it truly been a motte and bailey. Lying to the south of another earthwork called the Stadium, which was thought to have been used for games and races in centuries past, the land is believed to have been under the plough for centuries. Indeed, sixteenth-century antiquary John Leland noted, 'There be now large feeldes, fruteful of corn, in the very places where the howsing of the town was; and in these feeldes yereley be founde in ploughing many coynes of sylver and brasse of the Romaine stampe – Ther also have been found sepulchres, aqaue ductus tessalata paviamenta &.c.' (Toulmin Smith, 1964). Although the raised platform and bowl-shaped depression of the Stadium hints at an oval-shaped ringwork, excavations in 1935 found the depression to be natural (*Yorkshire Archaeological Journal*, 1959). In 1963 a survey suggested that 'Studforth Hill is a ploughed-out motte, probably the Vetus Burgus of the Pipe Rolls 1205–6 (and Rot. Chart 44).' (Renn, 1973). It wasn't until 2011 that Cambridge archaeologists ended centuries of speculation when a geophysical survey revealed a 'lost' Roman amphitheatre crowning the summit of the hill. The oval arena would have afforded a magnificent 360-degree view, making it the equivalent of a national theatre of the north.

ALMONDBURY

Undoubtedly one of the most prominent of Yorkshire's landmarks is at Castle Hill, Almondbury, just to the south of Huddersfield. The steep-sided promontory stands some 300m above the valley and dominates the landscape. The Victorian tower (erected to celebrate Queen Victoria's Diamond Jubilee in 1897) is popular with visitors for its fine, panoramic views, but not many realise that a motte and bailey castle once stood where it now stands. The man-made defences here actually date back to the early Iron Age. Indeed, excavations show that the summit has been occupied for more than 4,000 years. The earliest fortifications have been traced to the western end and continued until eventually the entire hilltop was filled with circular dwellings and multiple lines of defences that included works in stone. The early Norman earthworks comprise a series of banks and ditches that are still visible around the periphery and would have capitalised on the existing Iron Age hill-fort workings. These banks and ditches would have been fortified with a wooden stockade. Similarly, the motte would have been crowned with a timber tower and a wooden palisade.

The entrance to the outer bailey would have been to the east, where it was separated from the inner bailey by a deep ditch. Similarly, a gateway permitting entrance to the inner bailey once stood where the road now leads to the modern buildings on the hill. An even deeper ditch separated the inner bailey from a further enclosure to the west, where the motte would have stood. There is no evidence to suggest that a stone keep ever existed, although several hewn stones were found in a well that was discovered during work on the Victoria monument foundations. Some massive wall foundations have also been found (Brooke, 1901).

The first Norman baron associated with Almondbury was Ilbert de Lacy, who was given the honour of Pontefract (formerly Kirkby) by the Conqueror and began work on the castle there. Almondbury was added to the honour later, but de Lacy's estates were forfeited in 1102. As there is no record of a royal castle being built at Almondbury, Henry de Lacy either founded it either before 1102 or after the family's property was restored. Alternatively, Ilbert's grandson (1106–1141) might have been responsible. There is a theory that King Stephen built it during his reign (1135–1154) and that no record was kept. Whatever the truth, the de Lacy family held on to the castle up to and including the reign of Edward I (1272–1307), when it belonged to the family's most illustrious member, Henry de Lacy, Earl of Lincoln. Upon his death in 1311, it passed by marriage to Thomas Plantagenet, Earl of Lancaster, but was forfeited following his rebellion in 1321. The honour then passed to John of Gaunt, Duke of Lancaster and subsequently to Henry of Lancaster, who ascended the throne in 1399. It remained Crown property until 1627, after which it reverted to private ownership. Precisely when the castle was destroyed or dismantled is unclear, but in the first year of the reign of Edward II (1307–1327) a record in Dodsworth's *MSS* refers to the *former* Castle of Almondbury, which suggests it had been dismantled, although at least a prison or dungeon still existed. The *Inquisition,* 1584 expressly states that the Castle, 'which in antient time was the chief mansion house or scite of the said manor', has now 'of long time since been utterly decayed' (Brooke, 1901).

The Jubilee Tower is open to visitors during school holidays and offers a splendid viewing platform, not only for even better views over the surrounding countryside but also to gain a better impression of the site.

AUGHTON

The tiny village of Aughton is a quiet backwater overlooking the floodplain of the River Derwent, just 7 miles northeast of Selby. At the western end of the village, the main street terminates in a gated green lane leading to All Saints Church, next to which are the remains of a former motte and bailey stronghold attributed to Nigel Fossard. As a subfeudary of the count of Mortain (King William's half-brother), Fossard held no less than 95 manors in Yorkshire; as Aughton was not his main caput, the Aughton stronghold might have been built to control a crossing on the Derwent. He died in 1120, but the castle was probably abandoned early in the thirteenth century in favour of a

All Saints Church, Aughton and the castle motte to its right.

Swollen by February meltwater, the River Derwent had reached the churchyard and the western edge of the castle earthworks.

nearby moated site when the lands passed to the de la Haye family. The lands eventually passed by marriage to the Aske family who in turn abandoned the moated manorhouse about 1645. The roughly square-shaped bailey, located immediately southeast of the motte, has been incorporated into the grounds of the adjacent Aughton Hall.

The importance of the site did not elude I'Anson. 'The motte and bailey castle of Aughton, which subsequently became the stronghold of the Askes, feudatories of the Fossards and Mauleys, stands well above the River Derwent and occupies a site of considerable strategic importance. The motte is placed on a square platform, which is itself encircled by a square ditch – a somewhat unusual arrangement. The bailey, which is completely isolated from the motte, is guarded by a ditch 40 feet wide and six feet deep.' Notwithstanding the well-elevated site referred to by I'Anson, when the author visited in February, winter flood waters had swelled the Derwent to the width of a small lake and the water was only a few feet from the site.

The Aske family later propelled Aughton to national fame in connection with the Pilgrimage of Grace. In 1536, Robert Aske

7

The northern extremity of the earthworks at Aughton, showing the extent of the flooding.

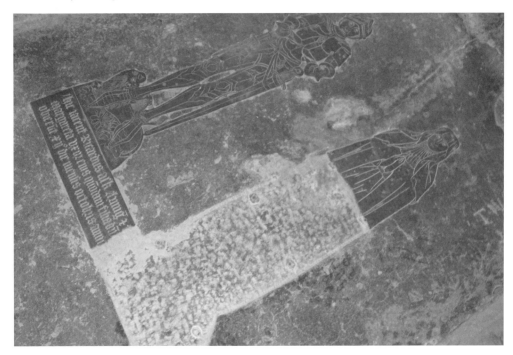

Brass effigies of Sir Richard and Lady Margaret Aske in All Saints Church.

became the reluctant leader of a vastly superior force of men (some 40,000 strong) from Lincolnshire and Yorkshire who objected to the religious reforms of the Crown (Henry VIII). Aske was tried, found guilty of treason and executed the following year. The uprising is still commemorated locally in an annual pageant. It is also worth looking inside the tiny, ancient All Saints Church, notable for its fine Norman arch, font and brass effigies of Sir Richard and Lady Margaret Aske. The keys can be obtained from the nearest (end) house in the main street. Nearby Aughton Hall now stands on the site of the original moated medieval manor house.

BARDSEY

Situated between Leeds and Wetherby, the attractive village of Bardsey cum Rigton claims to have not only officially the oldest pub in England (The Bingley Arms) but also the first Anglo-Saxon church tower in England (All Hallows), reputedly built between 800 and 825 AD. Overlooking the village is Castle Hill, on which stand the remains of a motte and bailey fortress attributed to Adam de Brus. In 1879, Clark wrote: 'Close north of the church, upon a knot of red sandstone, is an eminence known as Castle Hill, a name which in this part of the country, is usually applied to a moated mound. The eminence, like the knoll which it crowns, may be natural, but it is scarped and entrenched by art. It is about 20 ft. high, and oval or oblong in figure, with traces of a circumscribing ditch. The western end is isolated from the main body of the mound by a cross cut, across which lies a narrow bank of earth or causeway. The aspect of the whole is by no means clear. It has some of the characteristics of a small British camp, but if so it has certainly been occupied and altered by some English lord.' Clark's reference to a moated mound has led to suggestions that the hill might indeed have been an island. In 1902, Speight wrote: 'The great earthwork has apparently been encompassed by water; the beck-bordered land around lying low and marshy. Some years ago while draining on the east or deepest side of the hill, a bed of loose earth and stones was come upon, about 7 or 8 yards wide. It gave one the impression that this was part of a filled-up trench or moat, which in all probability in ancient times was carried round the hill. If such were the case, this circumvesture of waters, partly natural, partly artificial, would give the hill quite the appearance of an island, to which circumstance the ancient name of Berdeseie or Bardesei, may possibly be due. Bard, Barda, and Berda are well-known Saxon and Norse personal names, which compunded with the Anglo-Saxon *ea, ey* (an island), would explain the word as Barda's Island. In Domesday Bardsey appears as "Beresleseie" (the Norman scribe having erroneously made "d" into an "l").'

Excavations carried out in the late nineteenth century and in 1930 showed that works in masonry had at one time existed on the site. In addition to the foundations of a square stone keep, late twelfth- and early thirteenth-century pottery was found. The lack of pottery from any other period suggests the fortress was only occupied for a limited period. This theory is reinforced by evidence of medieval ridge-and-furrow ploughing in an area where the bailey was once situated, indicating the site had reverted to agriculture a long time ago.

Adam de Brus probably built the castle soon after being granted the manor of Bardsey in or about 1175 in a forced exchange for his estates in Danby, North Yorkshire. The lands were finally returned to Adam's son, Peter, in exchange for the West Riding lands and a payment of 1,000 pounds sterling, at which point Bardsey reverted to the Crown. The castle was presumably abandoned when the land passed to the monks of Kirkstall Abbey. Speight said, 'Though we possess no actual record of the transfer, it would appear that Bardsey and Collingham with Micklethwaite had been granted by the Crown before 1108 to Robert de Brus, whose grandson, Adam de Brus, by his marriage with Ivetta de Arches, succeeded to the manors of Thorp Arch and Walton. Robert de Brus, about the time named, exchanged these manors of Bardsey and Collingham for the vill and manor of Danby in Cleveland, together with lands at Gransmoor &c., in the East Riding. About the middle of the 12th century Bardsey and Collingham were in the hands of the Mowbrays. They bestowed these lands on Kirkstall Abbey.' Reverend Atkinson (1814–1900) also refers to the forced exchange of the de Brus lands in his book *Forty Years in a Moorland Parish*: 'Dugdale states that King Henry II "took the Castle of Danby, with Lordship and Forest thereto appertaining, and gave him instead thereof the Grange of Micklethwait, with the whole fee of Collingham and Berdsey," from Adam de Brus, son of Robert, the founder of the family and of the priory of Guisborough. To the statement as made by Dugdale, Ord (History of Cleveland, p. 248) adds that Adam by "adhering to Stephen throughout his stormy and disastrous career, had incurred the displeasure of Henry II," who thereupon acted in the way just named.'

Revered Atkinson also points us towards the date of the reversion of Bardsey to the Crown: 'In support and illustration of the foregoing, or some parts of it, I append the following translation of a document which I do not think has ever been much noticed before, and certainly at no great length by either of the former historians of Cleveland. It is from the Rotuli de Oblatis, p. 109, and under date 1200: "Peter de Brus has restored and quit-claimed to our Lord the King and his heirs for ever, the vills of Berdsey and Colingham and Rington, with all their appurtenances, as well in advowsons of churches, as in demesne lands, fees, homages, services, reliefs, and in all other matters to the said vills pertaining, without any reserve, in exchange for the vill of Daneby with all its appurtenances, and the forest of Daneby, which the King has restored to the said Peter and his heirs, to be held by him and his royal heirs by the service of one knight, in lieu of the aforesaid vills which King Henry, the father of the now king, had formerly given to Adam de Burs, the father of the said Peter, in exchange for the said vill and forest of Daneby."'

BARWICK-IN-ELMET

Situated roughly halfway between Leeds and Tadcaster, the ancient village of Barwick-in-Elmet is a place of special character and historic interest. It enjoys a splendid rural setting and has the distinction of being one of few places associated by name with the ancient Celtic kingdom of Elmet, which later became the West Riding of Yorkshire. Barwick has been occupied since the Iron Age and is thought to have been the capital and chief stronghold of Elmet. The earthworks of an Iron Age hillfort from this period exist on two adjacent hills near the centre of the village. To the north is Wendel Hill, named after Edwin, Earl of Mercia, a Saxon who once had his seat here. To the south is

Hall Tower Hill, which in addition to the hillfort earthworks also has the twelfth-century remains of a motte and bailey fortress attributed to Ilbert de Lacy. The motte is reputedly the largest in the West Riding. In medieval times, Barwick-in-Elmet belonged to the honour of Pontefract and was one of many manors bestowed upon Ilbert de Lacy by the Conqueror. Barwick later became the caput, or regional administrative centre, for the northern part of the honour following the decline of Kippax. The early Norman earthwork lies within the southern half of the Iron Age hillfort and some of its features were only discovered as recently as 1960 during building work. Excavations on this site have also turned up Roman coins, which are the oldest archaeological finds to date.

Hall Tower Hill and the adjacent, more northerly Wendel Hill were originally joined to form a single hill until the Norman period. Finding the 15-acre area within the Iron Age fort too large for the motte and bailey fortress he planned to build, de Lacy simply reduced the area of the bailey, consequently creating two hills. A street named The Boyle now occupies the place where the hill was bisected and the motte of de Lacy's fortress still stands in Hall Tower Field. Before the division, the whole site was encircled by a singe ditch and bank, but this is now partly obscured by modern housing. The deepest section can be traced on the northwestern side of Hall Tower Field, which is visible from a public footpath. In Norman times the defences were reworked and strengthened. The rampart to the side overlooking Rake Beck, as well as the bank and ditch on the eastern side, are attributed to this period. A massive inturned entrance on the northwest side of Wendel Hill is thought to be the original gateway to the Iron Age fort. Excavations in the 1800s uncovered skeletons, but no works in masonry have been found to date. A more recent geophysical survey also drew a blank regarding traces of building foundations in the bailey, which leads one to conclude that the fortress never developed beyond the earth and timber stage. Precisely when the fortress was abandoned is unclear, but the de Lacys held the honour for most of the Middle Ages before it eventually passed to the dukes of Lancaster and is still connected with that duchy today.

Hall Tower Field is open to the public, with access via a gate near a small chapel at the corner of Elmwood Lane. There is also a public footpath leading from The Boyle to the northern edge of Wendel Hill. The path leads to the corner of Meadow View, where there is a good view of the eastern defences. A circular route is achievable by turning right down Meadow View and following a narrow passage leading back to the earthworks. Turning right again brings you back to The Boyle via Maypole View. The footpath along the northwest section of the rampart offers great views over the surrounding countryside.

BOWES

Administratively, Bowes falls within the county of Durham, but historically it falls within the county boundary of the North Riding of Yorkshire. Located 4 miles southwest of Barnard Castle amid magnificent scenery, the village is located at the junction of two Roman roads where a fort once guarded the eastern entrance to a pass through the Pennines on the route between York and Carlisle. As one of the few upland passes between England and Scotland, its strategic importance came to the fore again in medieval times when in 1136, Alan de Bretagne, Count of Brittany erected a timber castle within the

The village of Bowes viewed from the northwest.

The twelfth-century stone keep at Bowes, as viewed from the churchyard. It was originally higher and the entrance was on the first floor.

One of two sculptures in the porch of he twelfth-century parish church of St Giles, which was extensively restored in 1863 (see opposite also).

ruins of the old Roman fort. Following the death without issue of Alan's son Conan in 1171, the castle passed to Henry II who spent the next few years strengthening it in stone due to military threat from Scotland. Henry's fears were well founded and a subsequent invasion and seige of the castle by King William's army took place in 1173. Saved by the approach of a relieving English force, the castle remained in the possession of the Crown until 1233, when Henry III gifted it to the duke of Brittany. It then changed hands several times and was latterly held by the powerful Neville family. In 1471 it once again reverted to the Crown, but was sold by James I in the early seventeenth century and largely dismantled after the English Civil War. In the ensuing years the site fell into disuse and in 1931 was gifted to the State by its last private owner, Lady Lorna Curzon-Howe. The castle ruins, of which only the twelfth-century rectangular keep remains,

The sculptures were possibly salvaged from the earlier building.

stand prominently in a field to the south of the main street and are clearly signposted by the 50ft-high keep. It offers fine views of open countryside, despite being encroached upon to the north by main-street houses. The keep was originally higher and entered from the east through a door at first-floor level. The moat remains unfilled to the south and east.

BRADFIELD
Situated 7 miles northwest of Sheffield and just within the Peak District National Park, the pleasant and unspoilt village of High Bradfield offers extensive views across Bradfield Dale towards Derwent Edge. Beyond the Church of St Nicholas on the northwest side of the village are the wooded and well-preserved earthworks known as Bailey Hill. Attributed to the de Furnivals, the fortress was possibly built to command the upper reaches of the River Loxley, or as an outlying stronghold for the earlier Sheffield Castle built in 1150 by William de Lovetot, holder of the manor of Hallamshire early in the twelfth century. Early Neolithic to late Bronze-Age finds at the base of the motte, including flint arrowheads, suggest that the site has pre-Norman origins.

The 10m-high, conical motte is defended by a wide ditch and is naturally protected by steeply sloping ground on the west, but has less defensible approaches on the south, east and least of all to the north. The triangular bailey to the south is protected by a rampart and deep ditch, but only a low bank remains on the steep western side. The wooded nature of the site makes viewing best in winter.

On the other side of the village, diametrically opposite to Bailey Hill, is the partial rectangular ringwork known as Castle Hill, which might also represent a medieval earth and timber fortress. Despite being a scheduled monument, the site could be a natural feature that simply appears man-made through the quarrying of stone.

BROMPTON
Travelling eastwards from Pickering along the A170 in the direction of Scarborough brings you to the interesting little village of Brompton, or Brompton-by-Sawdon to give the parish its proper name. Inventor

and aviation pioneer Sir George Cayley lived at Brompton Hall and poet William Wordsworth married here at All Saints Church in 1802. The site of the former motte and bailey castle is hidden from view to the immediate south of the high street, but is easily accessed via Cayley Lane, next to The Cayley Arms (sadly closed when the author visited). In I'Anson's day, the earthworks were unexcavated, but his keen eye quickly identified a mutilated motte and also signs of masonry foundations. A geophysical survey carried out in 2014 on behalf of the local history society confirmed features commensurate with structural activity. Writing more than 100 years before I'Anson, philanthropist and antiquary Thomas Hinderwell (1744–1825) mentioned that the foundations of an ancient castle were visible on 'Castle Hill' and that there was a local tradition that a fortress had indeed stood here. 'The foundations of an ancient building are still visible on an eminence called Castle-Hill, now surrounded by some venerable pines planted by the late Sir George Cayley, Bart.' Today the site is indicated as a castle mound on Ordnance Survey maps, but

The Castle Hill site at Brompton is put to good use as grazing land.

Looking west towards Cayley Hall from the top of Castle Hill, Brompton.

Castle Hill, Brompton, from the southwest.

18

it has been suggested that the hillock was merely the site of a siege castle dating from the reign of King Steven (1135–1154). The site has been heavily compromised by a defensible stone manor and is indeed listed as a fortified house. It is encroached upon to the north by houses and the author is grateful to an adjacent house owner for permitting photography (see opposite).

Little is known of the castle's history, but as Berenger de Todeni held the manor as part of his honour of Settrington (to the southeast of Malton) at the time of the Domesday Book and as there were no signs of remains of a castle at any of the other manors held by him in the North Riding, I'Anson suggested the earthworks at Brompton (Brunton Gamel in the Domesday Book) might be the location of his stronghold. Following his death (before 1115–1118) without an heir, de Todeni's wife remarried and the honour passed to her new husband, Robert de L'Isle. I'Anson learnt in a letter from antiquary William Farrer (1861–1924) that Brompton was subsequently granted to the Clere family from Norfolk, who also had property in Hampshire but whose main stronghold was in nearby Sinnington. Ownership subsequently passed to Eustace FitzJohn and finally to the Vescy family, together with the manors of Westhorpe and Snainton.

BURTON-IN-LONSDALE

Nestled on a hillside above the River Greta on the fringe of the Yorkshire Dales lies the quiet village of Burton-in-Lonsdale, which has been called 'the first and the last village in Yorkshire'. Once home to a thriving country pottery industry, the village became known locally as 'Black Burton' due to the smoke from the coal-fired kilns. Commanding superb views over the surrounding countryside and dominating the western approach to the village is Castle Hill, originally the site of an earth and timber ringwork fortress that was erected here in the late eleventh century, possibly to command a ford on the River Greta. Sources are divided on precisely who founded the castle: some attribute it to Robert de Mortain and others to Nigel de Albini, or possibly his son, Roger de Mowbray. However, it was developed into a motte and bailey castle during the reign of Henry I and grew in strategic importance under the ownership of the Mowbray family, who at the time held extensive lands in North West Yorkshire and Lancashire. By 1298 the family had relinquished much of their land in and around Burton, which became divided among a number of powerful Yorkshire families. It is not known for certain when the site was abandoned, but it has been suggested that this occurred during the reigns of Edward II or Edward III – sometime between1322 and 1369.

This fine example of a motte and bailey castle is characterised by its breastwork wall, which it still maintains around the upper part of the motte. An almost square bailey is evident to the west of the motte where the inner ditch, which would have completely encircled it, is also visible. A much smaller, half-rounded bailey exists to the south and there is a raised platform to the east where a farmyard now exists. Excavations in 1904 showed that paving was applied to the entire castle and some stonework can still be seen through the grass. In 1905, White wrote, 'Digging invariably disclosed a paved surface, both in the base-court, upon the embankments, under the sod, as well as upon the breastworks of the motte, and in the bottom of the moats. A face of stones appears to have coated the whole of the fortification, which must, before the growth of the turf, have presented a powerful and striking appearance.' Excavations of the motte further revealed a paved cavity edged by larger stones that represented the original earthwork forming the core of the larger mound visible today. Finds showed that the site was occupied long before the Normans arrived. 'It is allowable, therefore, to believe that in this "motte" we have specimens of more than one type of earthwork, the handiwork of races divided by the space of a great many years. The finds bear out this view,' continued White, referring to finds suggesting ancient British and even earlier occupation. 'A bone needle, flint arrowhead, and presumed burial cavities carry the mind back into very distant times – at least far beyond the period represented by the hill-structure as it presents itself to us at the present day.' Documentary evidence (*Pipe Rolls*, Henry I) supports the site's occupation by the Normans, but this was put beyond doubt by the excavations and finds of Norman workmanship, including Henry II 'first coinage', iron arrowheads and knives, a large key and a well-preserved (battle?) axe (White, 1905).

BUTTERCRAMBE

Buttercrambe is a small village in the Ryedale district of North Yorkshire, 7 miles east of York and just 2 miles north of Stamford Bridge. Situated amid beautiful scenery in this sleepy hamlet overlooking the River Derwent are the very mutilated remains of what was once a site of considerable strategic importance, for it was the stronghold of the de Stutevilles, or D'Estotevilles, who figured prominently in the annals of Norman England. Robert de Stuteville had accompanied the Conqueror to England at the conquest and received lands that had been confiscated from Torbrand, a pre-conquest Anglo-Saxon landowner whom the Conqueror evicted. Other prominent family members were Robert (died 1183), who was the benefactor of several great northern abbeys during the reign of Henry I, and his brother William who succeeded him.

The castle earthworks are in Aldby Park, which is private land connected with Aldby Hall and occupies the highest point in the village on the steep west bank of the Derwent. The grounds were much altered over the years, the grassy terracing being contemporary with sixteenth-century horse-breeding activities. The earthworks comprise two mounds linked by a rampart, and l'Anson believed they formed part of the bailey. The site has origins that are actually much older than the early Norman period. It has been occupied since Romano-Saxon times and is, no less, the place where Paulinus converted King Edwin of Northumbria to Christianity in the seventh century AD.

Egelfride once held the land here, but at the time of the Domesday Book it had passed to Hugh FitzBaldric, upon whose death it passed to Robert de Stuteville. Historian William Farrer (1861–1924) speculated that the fortress at Buttercrambe was built about 1090 and that the original castle of the de Stutevilles was probably located at Langton in the East Riding. Unhappily, the de Stutevilles' lot was not entirely without setbacks. In 1106 they were imprisoned for their support of Robert, Duke of Normandy in a plot against Henry I. Their lands were subsequently confiscated and later given to Nigel de Albini, the father of Roger de Mowbray. William, Robert de Stuteville's son, who was a principal commander at the Battle of the Standard, regained at least some of the lands, including Buttercrambe. But the theory that they were never entirely recovered is strengthened by the fact that the grandson of William still claimed property from William de Mowbray in the year 1200. If the original timber castle was ever developed in stone, it was probably during this period (I'Anson).

The property remained in the de Stuteville family until Joan, daughter of Nicholas de Stuteville, married Hugh Wake. In 1276 it passed to her son, Baldwin Wake, and was eventually inherited by Margaret, daughter of Ralph Neville, Earl of Westmorland, from whom the Darley family bought it in 1557. In 1582, Camden wrote that an old castle ruin was still visible on the top of the hill at Buttercrambe. A building (now demolished) was erected in the Tudor period slightly to the east of the present hall, which surely accounts for the disappearance of any remaining masonry from the de Stuteville fortress.

CARLTON-IN-COVERDALE

Coverdale, which lies in the eastern part of the Yorkshire Dales National Park to the south of Wensleydale, is a tributary valley of the River Ure just above Jervaulx Abbey. Extending from the bleak slopes of Coverhead in the west to the historic market town of Middleham in the east, Coverdale is one of the most picturesque of the Upper Dales. At Carlton, a village some 22 miles to the northwest of the market town of Ripon, are the remains of an eleventh-century fortress built by Ribald de Rufus.

Carlton is believed to have been an outpost of the more formidable fortress at Middleham, which later became the northern stronghold of Richard III. Indeed, an ancient road runs to the vale via Carlton from Middleham. Although there is uncertainty as to the origins and history of this site, I'Anson suggested it could have been built simply for the shelter of a few retainers to protect shepherds and pasturage rights in the vale of Kettlewell. There is no evidence that Carlton was ever more than a timber fortress.

The Domesday Book states that Bernulf owned the land at that time, but according to Farrer, his manors were subsequently granted to Ribald de Rufus, who was an ancestor of the FitzRandolphs. This

The motte at Carlton is behind the Foresters Arms.

Carlton is surrounded by majestic moorland scenery.

family had extensive pasturage rights in the locality and it is assumed it was necessary to protect them by means of an outpost. Situated on private land, the site overlooks majestic moorland and can easily be viewed from a public right of way behind the Foresters Arms. The conical-shaped motte has a flat top and is surrounded by a ditch that would once have been fed by the nearby stream. An ancient lime kiln that reputedly dates back to Roman times can also be found next to the motte.

CASTLE LEAVINGTON

Perched high above the River Leven amid pleasant rural scenery and presenting fine views of the Cleveland and Hambledon Hills, are the ruins of Castle Leavington. Lying close to the village of Middleton-on-Leven, just to the east of the A19 between Thirsk and Middlesbrough, this splendid fortress is strategically positioned on top of a steep headland protected on the eastern and northern sides by the river. Well defensible on account of the steep slopes on all sides except to the west and south, the site comprises a motte with no bailey. This is despite ample adjoining land that would have suited this purpose.

The large circular motte has a rampart that was so well preserved when I'Anson viewed it that he thought it must have a stone core underneath the earth. This assumption was based on the findings of a motte excavation made at Burton-in-Lonsdale. Due to the lack of a bailey, he further assumed that stabling for horses was underneath the tower, which would have been a formidable size in view of the area available within the palisade. Protected by a main ditch that completely encircles the 10m-high motte, there is also a very narrow crescent-shaped area with its own ditch some 3m below the top of the motte on the sides that were most likely to be attacked due to the lack of a bailey. In I'Anson's view, this proved that a bailey had never existed and he estimated the entrance would have been close to the edge of the precipice on the southeast.

The Crown owned the land at the time of the Domesday Book. At some late stage in the Conqueror's reign, or that of his son Rufus, it was granted to Robert de Brus, a baron who came over from Normandy at that time. de Brus had been granted other lands in

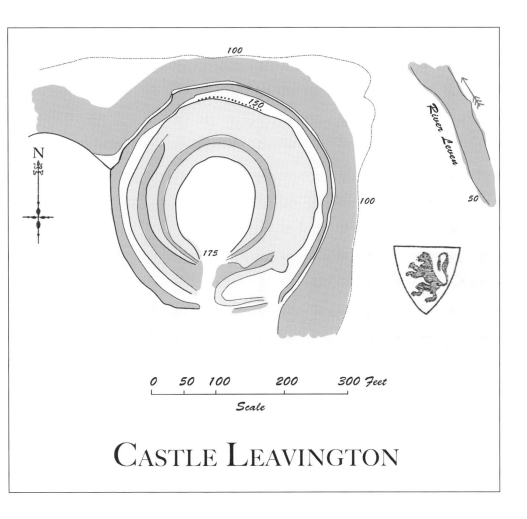

CASTLE LEAVINGTON

Cleveland and I'Anson suggested the castle was probably erected early in the reign of Stephen (1135–1154) during that period of civil war. It is thought that the castle was dismantled some time before 1274 (by order of Henry II). Henry divested Adam de Brus of his lordship of Danby and his fortress at Castleton in 1271, so I'Anson argued that he was probably forced to do the same at Leavington.

The manor and castle eventually passed to Nicholas de Meynell, Lord of Whorlton, who is thought to have rebuilt it in 1290. His eldest son and heir then occupied it for some time, followed in turn by his eldest daughter and his second son. It ultimately passed to Alice, his granddaughter, who married three times: firstly to William de Percy of Kildale, secondly to Robert de Boulton and thirdly to Walter de Boynton. When de Boynton died in 1391 or 1392, the castle reverted to the son of her first husband and finally to his sister, beyond which date it appears not to have been inhabited.

I'Anson was confident that the castle never developed any defences in masonry and that the building work carried out in 1290 by Nicholas de Meynell (referred to in Brown's *Yorkshire Inquisitions*) was simply a reconstruction of the old de Brus fortress.

CASTLETON

Situated in the North York Moors National Park, the site of the former fortress of Castleton stands sentinel high above the upper River Esk and amid wild moorland scenery reminiscent of the wilds of Scotland. Castle Hill is in the northeastern part of the village of Castleton, which lies approximately halfway between Castle Leavington and Whitby on the east coast. Although this is a motte castle without a bailey, a modern private dwelling on the motte disguises its proportions. Even 100 years ago, I'Anson referred to 'a modern farmstead' existing on the summit, which was presumably demolished to make way for the present building. In his book *Forty Years in a Moorland Parish*, Canon J.C. Atkinson (1814–1900), the former vicar of Danby, gives an excellent account of the history of these parts, including the castle and lordship of Danby.

The castle motte is shaped roughly like a horseshoe, but due to the defacement, further details can only be assumed. Considering the size and thickness of the foundations (Atkinson estimated the northern curtain wall to have been 13ft thick and 11ft thick on the east side and around the northeast angle), I'Anson imagined a shell keep with a great hall to have stood here with windows on the courtyard or inward side. The rampart, which would have been topped by a stockade, terminates in a small hillock to the southwest and I'Anson speculated that this was the platform for a small tower overlooking the entrance. He further suggested that an identical tower originally existed on the other side of the entrance, but that this would have been destroyed when the

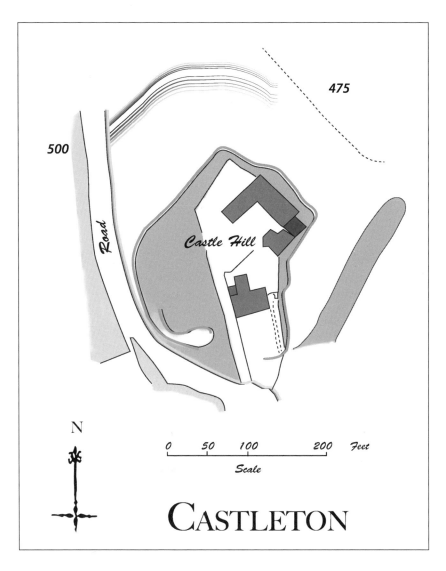

475

500

Road

Castle Hill

N

0   50   100   200   *Feet*

Scale

CASTLETON

modern building was erected. This tower arrangement supports his argument that a bailey probably never existed.

Although Castleton appears to have been a small but strong fortress, the site was once much larger. Originally, it occupied a considerable area but was cut through by the road to the station and the foundations for the Primitive Methodist chapel, which have dissected the original

An impression of the original fortress at Castleton.

moat on that side. The earth mound on the castle side of the road is in no small part due to the removal of soil to accommodate these relatively modern innovations. Atkinson thought that few people were even aware of the former existence of a castle at the time, making it a case of defacement through ignorance, rather than a lack of respect for all things ancient.

Gamel and subsequently his son, Orm, were the pre-Conquest lords of the land in these parts, but at the time of the Domesday Book, Hugh FitzBaldrick held the lordship and forest of Danby. When he died about 1089, the lordship was given to Robert de Brus (from which the anglicised name of Robert the Bruce is derived). This grant of lands in Cleveland by Rufus was thought to be in exchange for other lands. The indications are that de Brus had the fortress built early in the reign of Rufus before he was given the lordship and castle of Skelton, which later became the caput of his barony. However, he had been a principal supporter of Stephen against Empress Matilda, which could have been why Henry II (in 1158) forced Adam de Brus to exchange the castle and manor for lands taken forcibly (by the Crown) from the monks of Kirkstall Abbey near Leeds. But in 1200, Castleton once again came into the possession of the de Brus family after Adam's son had succeeded him. In 1271 the lordship and land passed to Marmaduke de Thweng of Kilton Castle by virtue of his wife Lucia, who was a co-heiress of Peter de Brus. But by this date the castle had deteriorated or might even have been in ruins. In 1294 it passed to William le Latimer junior, who had married Lucia. William abandoned the castle c.1300 and built Danby Castle, a quadrangular palace-fortress that lies a short distance away on the Danby estate. While you are in the Castleton area, a small detour eastwards will lead you to the remains of Danby Castle, which although greatly modified, still give a good impression of how it must have looked before it was dismantled. Acquired by the Dawnay family in the mid-seventeenth century and still inhabited by them, Danby Castle lies at the foot of Danby Rigg on the moors escarpment just 2 miles southeast of Castleton. You will not fail to be enchanted by its romantic setting and the views across Eskdale.

Wild moorland scenery surrounds Castleton in upper Eskdale.

CATTERICK

Nestled strategically between the old Roman road of Dere Street and the River Swale, some 8¹/₂ miles northwest of North Yorkshire's county town, Northallerton, the village of Catterick dates back to Roman times when it was known as Caractonium, from the Latin word *cataracta* meaning 'waterfall' or 'portcullis' (although some suggest that the Romans merely misunderstood the Celtic name *Catu-rātis* meaning 'battle ramparts'). The castle motte is in the village centre, immediately north of St Anne's Church, but there is no mention of it in any record. I'Anson wrote, 'The motte, if motte it be, which Gale calls "Mons Palatinus", is a small one lying immediately north of the church and the supposed bailey, and is now known as "Palet Hill." The present churchyard, which occupies a triangular promontory, certainly presents every appearance of having been the bailey of a Norman earth-and-timber castle. It is defended by steep natural slopes, which would seem to have been scarped away, and the ditch on the west is of great depth.'

That there is no record was of no surprise to I'Anson, who reasoned it was probably founded by Count Alan the Black of Richmond as a temporary measure taken during the civil warfare at the time of Stephen. Similar fates of other castles founded by Alan the Black had fortunately been recorded at other castle sites covered in this book, namely Yafforth and Hutton Conyers. I'Anson continued: 'By the merest chance we happen to possess records which prove the history of Yafforth and Norton Conyers, neither of which are, in appearance, such typical sites for a Norman stronghold as is Catterick… . If these records did not happen to exist, both would have been more doubtful Norman castles than is Catterick.'

Visitors to Catterick (or Ravensworth and Grinton for that matter) will find themselves tantalisingly close to Richmond, home to one of Yorkshire's great tourist attractions. Richmond Castle, the formidable stone edifice attributed to Alan le Roux (c.1071), commands fine views over the Swale valley and beyond. It is only omitted from this book because it has never been an earth and timber fortress. 'Owing to the strategic importance of the site selected, only one great castle was needed by Count Alan, and consequently he was in a position to lavish upon that one structure all the labour and material which another baron, of equal but scattered estates, would have to spend on the erection of ten or a dozen castles,' wrote I'Anson.

CONISBROUGH

The town of Conisbrough lies midway between Doncaster and Rotherham in South Yorkshire. High above the town stand the formidable and iconic remains of Conisbrough Castle. Made famous by novelist Sir Walter Scott, the ruins had become a major attraction by the end of the nineteenth century and so it might seem an odd choice for a book about 'secret' castles. But this ancient seat of the earls of Warenne had humble beginnings as an earth and timber fortress, which is why it receives a mention. William de Warenne, 1st Earl of Surrey and son-in-law of William the Conqueror, built the original castle on or about 1170. But when William, 3rd Earl of Surrey died in 1147 without a male heir, the fortress passed by marriage to Hamelin Plantagenet, the illegitimate son of Henry II, who rebuilt the castle in stone in the late twelfth century. It remained in the family until the death of John de Warenne in 1347, when it reverted to the Crown. Edmund of Langley, Duke of York was then gifted the castle by his father, Edward III, and the castle remained in the family until 1446. Richard, Duke of York was next to gain possession, but he was killed in 1460 at the Battle of Wakefield, upon which his son, Edward (later crowned Edward IV), inherited. It remained a royal castle until Elizabeth I granted it to her cousin, Henry Carey, and remained in private hands before eventually falling into ruin, which was why it played no part in the English Civil War. In 1737 the castle was bought by the Duke of Leeds and in 1859 sold to Sackville Lane-Fox, 12th Baron of Conyers, in whose family it remained until English Heritage acquired it in 1949. The town has a building even more ancient than the castle: the Anglo-Saxon Church of St Peter. Dating back to the eighth century, the church is claimed to be the oldest building in South Yorkshire and is located immediately to the southwest of the castle.

COTHERSTONE

This remote outpost – at least as far as Yorkshire's secret castles are

The earthworks at Cotherstone are best viewed from the south.

The path beyond the site leads to a delightful view of the Tees valley.

concerned – is situated in the Pennine hills next to the confluence of Balder Beck and the River Tees. Although the village now lies within the boundary of County Durham (it was transferred for administrative and ceremonial purposes on 1 April 1974), historically it was part of North Yorkshire and so receives a mention. 'The ancient fortress of the Fitz-Hughs – which, like Castleton, was a motte castle devoid of a bailey – stands on the angle of a height to the north of the village of Cotherstone, amid beautiful scenery, about four miles north-west of Barnard Castle,' wrote I'Anson. Founded by Bodin, son of Eudo, Count of Penthievre in Brittany, early in the reign of Rufus (c.1090), it might have been erected to defend Teesdale, possibly at the request of Bodin's overlord, Alan the Black. Excavations have revealed fragments of burnt wood that suggest the original timber fortress might have been destroyed by plundering Scots, although an accidental fire

Hallgarth Hill falls away sharply to the north where it descends into the Tees valley.

Masonry fragments visible in the walls of an adjacent house built in the mid-eighteenth century were most likely rescued from the castle ruins.

can't be ruled out. It was strengthened in masonry by Henry FitzHervey about 1200 (licence granted in 1201), and masonry fragments still exist, including the footings of a two-winged building of a later date. There are also traces of formal gardens and fishponds.

In his latter years, Bodin became a monk at St Mary's Abbey in York, at which point the castle passed to his brother, Bardulf, who eventually followed him into the same order at St Mary's. His son, Akarius FitzBardulf (founder of Fors Abbey in Wensleydale), succeeded him at Cotherstone and the castle subsequently passed to Herveius (or Hervey), the son of Akarius. Hervey died in 1182 and was succeeded by Henry FitzHervey.

The site is on private land to the immediate northeast of the village, just a short distance down a narrow lane opposite the Fox & Hounds public house, and is best reached on foot. Take the right fork of the lane up the incline of Hallgarth Hill and the earthworks lie behind the row of cottages on the left. A friendly owner kindly gave access to the land at the back for a better view and the public right of way beyond the site to the north offers an excellent view of the Tees valley. If the Fox & Hounds is closed, refreshments are available at the village's friendly Brook House (Yorkshire tea, of course).

COTTINGHAM

A large village situated to the immediate northwest of Kingston upon Hull, Cottingham is home to the site of what was known (at least since the nineteenth century) as Baynard Castle. The first record of a building on the site dates from the 1170s, but pottery finds suggest that a Saxon settlement might have existed here. The large site (the inner bailey alone measured roughly 90m by nearly 100m) was encircled and severely encroached upon by housing development in the twentieth century, but still has traces of a rampart and moat. It is hidden from public view by the houses fronting West End Road and the western end of Northgate. Attributed to Robert de Stuteville, whose son William was granted a licence to fortify the manor house in 1201, the manor and castle subsequently passed by marriage to the de Wake family and then the Holland family before being divided into three separate manors in 1407.

The castle has received at least one royal visit and caught the attention of the monarchy on more than one occasion. In 1896, Mackenzie wrote: 'About three miles from Beverley stood this old 12th-century fortress of the Stutevilles and Wakes. Robert de Stuteville was Sheriff of Yorkshire in 21 Henry II, and is said to have built the castle. His descendant, William, who was here in John's reign, quarrelled with the churchmen at York, and was excommunicated by the archbishop; and the king, with a fellow feeling, paid him a visit to inquire into the matter, which ended in a victory for the layman, and permission granted to fortify his house. William's great-granddaughter, Joan, brought the manor and the castle to her husband, of the de Wake family, and her son, Baldwin de Wake, inherited these and many other lands. In 1319, Thomas de Wake, obtained a charter of confirmation, and a further licence to convert his manor-house into a castle of defence, under the name of Baynard's Castle, with authority to keep it armed and garrisoned, which patent was renewed by Edward III, on his accession. The vast property of the Wakes then came to royal hands, by the marriage of Edmond of Woodstock, youngest son of Edward I, to Margaret, the sister of Thomas de Wake; she bore him a daughter, Joan, the Fair Maid of Kent, who had as her first husband, the warrior Thomas, Earl of Holland, and after his early death held the manor of Cottingham and its dependencies; afterwards becoming the wife of the Black Prince, she was the mother of King Richard II. Nothing is known as to the description of the buildings which composed this castle. It was burnt to the ground in the reign of Henry VIII, and was never rebuilt. There is a story given by Allen, but scarcely worthy of belief, that the Lord Wake during that period himself caused his house to be destroyed by fire, to prevent the coming thither of the king, whose power and fascination he dreaded on behalf of his beautiful wife. The last Wake dying s.p., the manor was divided into three parts, in favour of his three daughters, who were married respectively to the Duke of Richmond, the Earl of Westmorland, and Lord Powis, and the names of these nobles are still attached to the properties. The area covered by the castle was about two acres, but nothing now remains to marke its site except the traces of the outer and inner moats and some banks.'

Thomas de Wake died in 1349 and if one rejects the story by Allen, the date when the castle was destroyed or abandoned is a matter of conjecture. Upon visiting the site in 1538, antiquarian John Leland found the castle in ruins. 'Entering into the South part of the great Uplandish Town of Cotingham, I saw where the Stutevilles Castelle, dobill dikid and mostid, stood, of the which nothing now remaynith.' And in 1590, William Camden described the castle as 'an ancient ruin utterly fallen into decay'. By the mid-seventeenth century, Charles I had sold off the Cottingham manors. The timber-framed house known as Sarum Manor (the grade II listed Old Manor House of today) is thought to have been one of the four houses noted by Leland on the site in 1538. A small-scale excavation in 1991 identified chalk floors, wall footings and metalworking areas with hearth bases all dating to between the twelfth and fourteenth centuries. Fragments of Middle

Saxon pottery were also uncovered, suggesting pre-Norman activity. There was a rampart around the moat and outer bailey, on which the houses along West End Road and the western end of Northgate were erected, but only a stretch of this outer bank, to the east of the eastern moat ditch, survives as undeveloped land.

CRAYKE

Situated at the foot of the Howardian Hills, midway between York and Helmsley, are the remains of the former motte and bailey fortress at Crayke, which stand in a lofty position amid pleasant countryside. According to I'Anson, the castle probably owes its origin to Ranulf Flambard (reign of Rufus), or Bishop Pudsey (1153–1195): 'This manor was a place of considerable historic importance for some time previous to the Conquest and long before Flambard or Pudsey erected the "castel" the Saxon bishops of Durham had an "aula" or manor house on the site.' The earliest reference to the timber castle was in 1195 when Pudsey stayed there en route from Durham to Howden where he died allegedly from an illness brought on by overindulgence at the table in Crayke. The first works in masonry were carried out between 1283 and 1310, with further major works between 1437 and 1457. The castle was dismantled in 1647 by order of Parliament and subsequently used as a farmhouse. The see of Durham remained lords of the manor until c.1830 and Crayke remained an outlying part of Durham until as late as 1844 (I'Anson).

All that remains visible of the motte is an earthwork (mound) to the north on which later buildings were constructed. The inner bailey occupied most of the Crown of the hill, as far as St Cuthbert's Church, but only a short section of the defences (a bank to the southeast) can still be seen. The present garden wall alongside Crayke Lane follows its extremity and the site is visible from the road.

CROPTON

The village of Cropton derives its name from the Anglo-Saxon for 'hill-top settlement' and lies a short distance to the northwest of Pickering on the most direct route to Rosedale Abbey. Overlooking the River Seven valley to the northeast of the village are the earthworks

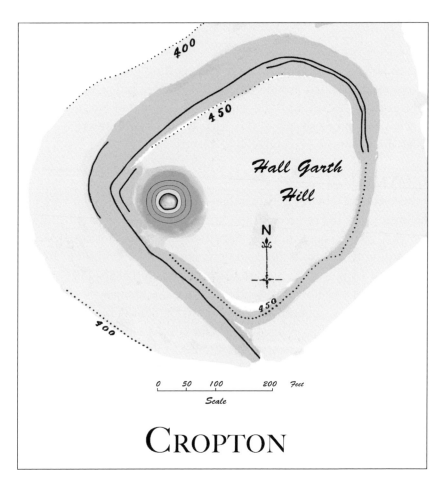

400

450

Hall Garth
Hill

N

450

400

| 0 | 50 | 100 | | 200 | Feet |

Scale

CROPTON

of the former fortress of the de Stutevilles. They lie in a field on a promontory known as Hall Garth Hill that would originally have offered an outstanding view of Rosedale. A modern plantation partially impedes the view today, although some tree felling has been carried out. To reach the site, simply follow the track to the right of St Gregory's church and after a short distance the earthworks appear.

The motte, which originally would have been crowned by a palisade, is located at the western end of a triangular bailey, but has suffered considerable silting down over the centuries. So much so that I'Anson considered it impossible to say what its exact dimensions had been when he viewed it more than a century ago. From the existence of the northern rampart ditch and a part of the southern rampart he estimated the bailey had covered an area of just over 3 acres.

According to the Domesday Book, Cropton manor belonged to the Crown, but early in the reign of Rufus it passed to Robert de Stuteville, who erected the fortress. The castle reverted to the Crown when Robert was captured at the Battle of Tinchebrai, but Henry II restored it to Robert's son William, who fought at the Battle of the Standard. The castle stayed in the de Stuteville family until the heiress of Nicholas de Stuteville married Hugh Wake. Between 1290 and 1295, Hugh's grandson John erected a half-timber manor house within the bailey to the east of the motte, but these are thought to be the only works in masonry that were developed at this site. By 1349 the fortress was in ruins.

Cropton Bank Wood, the wooded area that falls away to the left from the castle site, is managed by the Woodland Trust and offers a circular walk for those feeling energetic. While you are at Cropton, you can also visit the remains of the former Roman fortress known as Cawthorne Camp, which involves a 2-mile detour. It comprises well-preserved earthworks located on what was an old Roman road between Malton and Dunsley Bay.

The earthworks at Cropton viewed from St Gregory's churchyard.

DONCASTER

The large and ancient market town of Doncaster developed around the site of a Roman fort (Danum) built in the first century at a crossing of the River Don. The settlement became an Anglo-Saxon burh and was refortified after the Norman Conquest by Nigel Fossard. It is thought that he built either a motte and bailey or a ringwork castle here, probably before 1068, and that Henry II ordered its destruction at the end of the Civil War (Buckland and Dolby, 1972). The passage of time has removed every visible trace of it, but the site of the castle was eventually located under the eastern end of St George's Church during excavations carried out in the early 1970s. These excavations also revealed that the castle had stood in the northeast corner of the old Roman fort and had been surrounded by a deep and wide ditch. An outer bailey ditch was also located, but all of these had been levelled by 1200. In 1986 part of the castle ditch was discovered during an archaeological evaluation of Frenchgate (South Yorkshire Sites and Monument Record).

Writing in 1603, antiquary William Camden mentioned the castle in his work *Britannia*: 'From hence Done, running with a divided streame hard to an old towne, giveth it his owne name, which we at this day call Dan-caster, the Scots Don-castle, the Saxons *Dona-ceaster*, Ninnius*Caer Daun*, but Antonine the Emperour Danum, like as the booke of *Notices*, which hath recorded that the Captaine of the Crispinian Horsemen lay there in garison under the Generall of Britaine. This about the yeere of our Lord 759 was so burnt with fire from heaven, and laie so buried under the owne ruines, that it could scarce breath againe. A large plot it sheweth yet, where a Citadell stood, which men thinke was then consumed with fire, in which place I saw the Church of S. Georges, a faire Church, and the onely Church they have in the towne.'

Likewise, in his *Itinerary* in or about the years 1535–1543, John Leland wrote, 'I notid these thinges especially yn the towne of Dancaster. The faire and large paroch chirche of St George, standing in the very area, where ons the castelle of the toune stoode, long sins clene decayid. The dykes partly yet be seene and the foundation of part of the waulles. There is a likelihood that when this chirch was erected much of the ruines of the castelle was taken for the fundation and the filling of the waullis of it.'

The medieval Church of St George was destroyed by fire in 1853 and the splendid Minster Church of Saint George now standing at the heart of the town was built between 1854 and 1858 to the designs of Sir George Gilbert Scott. English poet and writer Sir John Betjeman once described it as 'Victorian Gothic at its very best.'

DRAX

Close to the River Ouse on the southern edge of the village of Drax, roughly 2 miles southeast of Selby, is Castle Hill Farm, where an earth and timber fortress attributed to Philip de Colville is reputed to have stood. We learn from William of Newburgh, writing in the twelfth century, that King Stephen visited York and that he decreed the demolition of a fortalice at Drax, which commanded navigation on the Ouse (Farrer, 1914): 'In the summer of 1154, Stephen made a royal progress to the north, and on the way caused the adulterine castles, which were a harbour for evil-doers and dens of thieves, to be destroyed by fire before his eyes. Upon coming into Yorkshire, he found Philip de Colevill, who had been ordered to set fire to his stronghold at Drax, in rebellion, and full of reliance as to the strength of his castle, the courage of his garrison, and the supply of food and weapons. The king, however, having summoned sufficient forces from the adjoining counties, besieged, assaulted and quickly overcame the castle, although it was almost inaccessible by reason of its surroundings of rivers, woods and marshes.'

Proof that a castle existed here is not in dispute. What is in dispute is the precise location. This is due to the site bearing no trace of a motte and being listed as a raised moated enclosure, making it more likely to be a fourteenth-century manorial dwelling rather than a twelfth-century castle. The site, which lies 350m to the south of   St Peter and St Paul's Church, is in an area that in the Middle Ages was marshy and sometimes recorded as being flooded. Trying to build a deep-ditched mound would have been extremely difficult due to constant water seepage. The suggestion that the site was inhabited in a pre-Norman period has also been made, although there is no evidence. A geophysical survey in 2006 detected a large number of anomalies indicating different kinds of ground disturbance. Much of this was thought to be modern, or relate to the different stages of construction of the farmhouse and outbuildings over the past few hundred years. However, it was not ruled out that certain anomalies might relate to earlier occupation. Some, for instance, corresponded to the infilled moat, but circular features on the southern edge of the moat were of unknown origin.

The uncertainty as to the true location of the site brings to mind the fortress at Hood (or Hod) Hill. In 1913, I'Anson wrote that he had been unable to locate any traces of earthworks. In 1970, Whitaker suggested that Hood Hill was the true site, which was later proven by excavations in 2000. Might the motte – if there was one at Drax – have been levelled and used as a platform on which to build the manor house? Perhaps the passage of time will once again provide an answer.

EASBY

The earthwork known as 'Castle Hill' occupies a dominant position on the North York Moors escarpment overlooking the River Leven and lies roughly a mile from the village of Easby, which is near Stokesley. The steep, almost vertical, gradient surrounding the site is heavily wooded and its situation resembles that of Castle Leavington. The exception is that the earthwork here, as at Castleton, is horseshoe-shaped due to the formidable natural defences. I'Anson suggested a timber keep would probably never have existed due to the small size of the motte, which would have been crowned with a palisade. There is no bailey, and excavations in 1903 revealed no masonry or other interesting finds. These excavations might account for the slight depression on the summit of the motte, but it was possibly caused by landslip, I'Anson thought.

Despite a theory that the motte might simply be a man-made mound associated with hunting, I'Anson favoured a connection with warfare: 'We know nothing whatsoever of the history of this Norman earthwork, but the probabilities are that it represents a castle erected during the civil wars of the time of Stephen by Bernard Balliol, the commander-in-chief of the Anglo-Norman army at the Battle of the

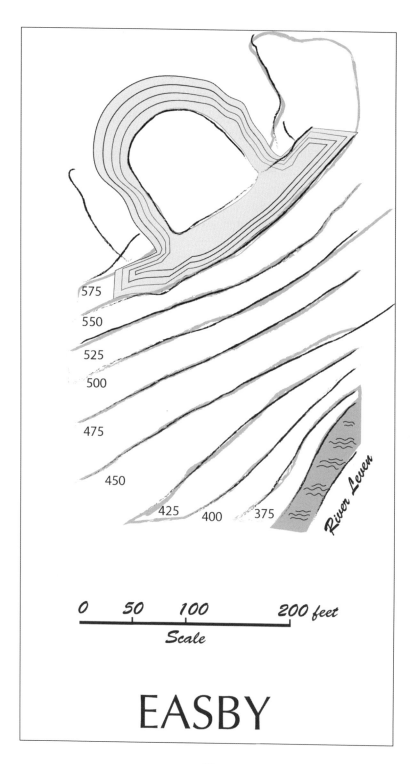

575
550
525
500
475
450
425 400 375

River Leven

0   50   100   200 feet
Scale

EASBY

Standard.' Bernard was the son of Guy de Balliol, who was granted the manor of Easby as part of the lordship of Stokesley. It was Bernard's great-grandson who became king of Scotland, so the theory probably holds that the castle was built to defend an outlying portion of the Balliol estates and that it was abandoned at some later stage when times grew more stable (I'Anson).

The site is on private land and heavily wooded. If you are in the Easby area and have not yet been to Kildale, it makes good sense to visit it next, as it is just 1½ miles away.

FELIXKIRK (or FELISKIRK)

The earthwork known as Howe Hill is in the centre of the village of Felixkirk, halfway between the North York Moors escarpment and the fine old market town of Thirsk. Officially listed as a Bronze Age barrow, the triangular earthwork is also thought to represent the site of a motte and bailey castle. Documentary evidence of this is non-existent, but I'Anson knew what he saw: 'Immediately to the north of the vicarage and some 150 yards south of the church in the pretty village of Feliskirk is what would certainly appear to be a small

The motte at Felixkirk as viewed from The Carpenters Arms.

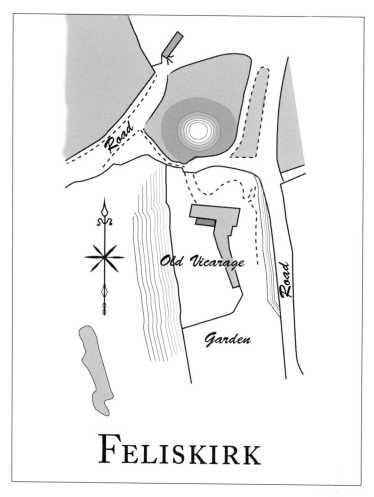

FELISKIRK

artificial motte.' Even in his day, crucial clues had already been obliterated. 'View the place from whatever point we like, it has every appearance of having been a motte and bailey castle, but the mutilation it has undergone renders it impossible to say definitely that such was the case. The vicarage garden looks very much like a bailey, but here again, what may have been the bailey ditch on the east is occupied by a road.'

I'Anson thought the castle might have been built by the powerful Fossards, who settled here as early as the reign of Henry I. This was supported in a letter to him from fellow antiquary William Farrer: 'Considering the proximity of the Fossard estates to the York–Durham road, there would be nothing surprising in the possession by the

The tomb and effigy of Sir William Cantilupe in the Church of St Felix, Felixkirk.

The tomb of Lady Cantilupe.

Fossards of a stronghold at Feliskirk.' Another fellow antiquary and author proposed a period when the castle might have been built: 'In his interesting description of this (Felixkirk) church, Mr. A. Hamilton Thompson, F.S.A., tells us that the probable date of the original portion of the church is "the first quarter of the twelfth century," which coincides with the advent of the Fossards of Feliskirk, and the probable erection of the castle, if castle there were.' Documented evidence (*Yorkshire Fines*) confirms that the Fossards either sold or donated their property here to the monastic houses of Byland and Newburgh, and to the Hospitallers of Mount St John in 1210.

While in Felixkirk, it is worth visiting the quaint Church of St Felix, which contains the tombs and effigies of Sir William and Lady Cantilupe. Sir William died in 1309. Those in need of refreshment will not find a more convenient hostelry than The Carpenters Arms, which is as close to the earthworks as it could possibly be – the width of the road skirting the motte.

FOSS (also known as LYTHE)
The remains of the former motte and bailey stronghold built by the Fossard family are most pleasantly situated in Mulgrave Woods near the village of Lythe, just to the west of Whitby. They stand on the northern bank of a tributary feeding Sandsend Beck, which rises on the North York Moors and flows towards the sea at Sandsend. Believed to be of Saxon origin, the site clearly inspired I'Anson when he visited it more than 100 years ago: 'At one point in the course of its career Sandsend Beck dashes through a narrow dingle or ravine, where picturesque rocks jut out like gargoyles, where ledges create beautiful waterfalls, and where the beck fights its way seawards, amid moss-grown rocks and hanging precipices overhung by ancient trees. On the left-hand side of this ravine, at the edge of the wood, are the tree-grown earthworks of Foss Castle.'

The circular motte is 40m wide on the top and is partially surrounded by a wide, deep ditch on all but the southern side where there is a sheer drop into the beck. To the west, the relatively small bailey was defended by a deep, broad ditch, which merges to the northwest with the main ditch around the motte. The banquette was

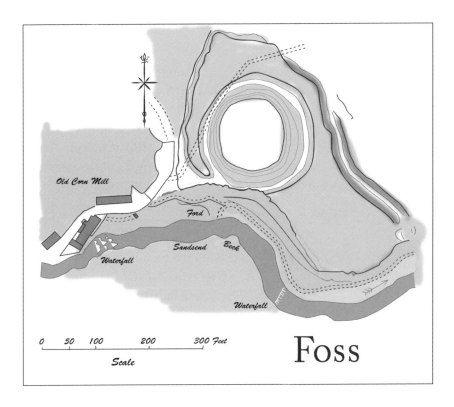

Old Corn Mill

Ford

Sandsend   Beck

Waterfall

Waterfall

0   50   100   200   300 Feet

Scale

Foss

mutilated at the beginning of the nineteenth century, but would originally have increased the height of the motte ramparts. I'Anson thought the original motte was crowned by a large timber tower with a great hall and private apartments and that later a new hall was probably built at the south end of the bailey.

Erected in 1072 by the great castle builder Nigel Fossard, the fortress at Foss was his Cleveland caput and just one of several attributed to him, others being Mount Ferrant, Lockington and Aughton (all in the East Riding) and Langthwaite near Doncaster. He died in or about 1091 and left at least three sons. Robert, his successor as feudal baron, had four sons and two daughters. William I, the third feudal baron, who succeeded him about 1135, was a principal commander at the Battle of the Standard. William Fossard II, the fourth feudal baron, succeeded him, but I'Anson suggests he might have been the grandson rather than the son of William I. In 1165 the estates passed to William le Gros, Earl of Albemarle, whose daughter Joan inherited and married Robert de Turnham, who was the armour bearer to Richard I. Robert abandoned Foss in or about 1197 when he built Old Mulgrave Castle, the rectangular-keep fortress just half a mile to the east of Foss.

Today, both ruins stand on land owned by the Mulgrave estate and public access is limited to Sundays. There are several entry points to Mulgrave Woods, but the footpath from Sandsend offers an agreeable walk.

GREAT DRIFFIELD

Situated on the southern fringe of the Yorkshire Wolds and close to the source of the River Hull, the ancient market town of Great Driffield was once a royal residence and thus considerably important. The *Anglo-Saxon Chronicle* records the death of King Alfrid of Northumbria, who was allegedly buried here in AD 705. Due to the abundance of tumuli or Danes' Graves in the vicinity, there is also a suggestion that the famous Battle of Brunanburh might have been fought at Battleburn, a few miles to the southwest of the town. What is certain, however, is that it was an important royal manor at various stages from the eleventh to the fifteenth centuries and that a motte and bailey castle existed at Moot Hill, not far from the town centre. The motte was mistaken for a Bronze Age round barrow in the nineteenth century, but excavations in 1975 confirmed it is of Norman origin, with evidence of late Roman occupation underlying it.

Attributed to Hugh d'Avranches, 1st Earl of Chester, the fortress is thought to have been built in or about 1086 and was refortified in the early thirteenth century. The motte, which was originally much larger than it is today, suffered damage from gravel quarrying operations in the mid-nineteenth century and the partial ditch surrounding it is still discernible. However, the bailey is difficult to identify. The site is on private land and obscured from view on all sides by modern housing. There is no record of when the fortress at Driffield was abandoned, but the d'Avranches family, which held land throughout western Normandy, was well rewarded by Duke William for contributing 60 ships to the invasion force and no doubt fighting with him at the Battle of Hastings. Hugh d'Avranches spent much of his time fighting the Welsh and stayed loyal to the Crown during the rebellion in 1088. He later

Moot Hill in Great Driffield has shown evidence of occupation since late Roman times.

served as a royal councillor at the court of Henry II and founded Benedictine abbeys in Normandy and Chester. Upon Hugh's death, his son Richard succeeded and when he died, the title passed to Hugh's nephew, Ranulph le Meschin, who was a commander at the Battle of Tinchebrai. Ranulph's son and heir, Ranulph de Gernon, inherited, but was poisoned in 1153. Henry III subsequently gave the manor to his sister Joan upon marrying Alexander, king of the Scots, after which it reverted to the Crown before passing to John de Balliol, king of Scotland. It was then forfeited, and remained with the Crown before being granted to the le Scrope family in 1336.

The site is entirely ring-fenced by housing, but the author found the most convenient viewing point to the back of the houses in Eastgate North. Interesting earthworks relating to Driffield's earlier royal settlement can also be seen in the nearby park across the road from Eastgate North.

GRINTON

The village of Grinton lies on the south bank of the River Swale in the Yorkshire Dales National Park, roughly 7 miles to the southeast of

Richmond. Famous for its splendid scenery, Swaledale is a walker's paradise. The name Grinton means literally 'the green pasture' in Old English and aptly enough this place is where the moorland meets the gentler land of the lower dale. The earliest reference to the village dates back to 1086, when Bodin held the manor here. Being the first place above Richmond where the river could be forded, the crossing point at Grinton would have been important in bygone times and it is not surprising that some kind of fortification should have existed there. The site might even date back to the Iron Age and is located on a glacial moraine in a pasture close to the River Swale to the east of the village. It essentially comprises two platforms separated by an artificially steepened hollow. The whole site covers an area of roughly 150m² and is enclosed by a bank and ditch. Although there are no traces of ancient buildings and indeed there are even doubts about whether or not the two platforms are contemporary, it is thought that both were selected for habitation during the medieval period.

View looking east (taken from the church tower) showing the earthworks at Grinton.

Splendid moorland scenery awaits visitors to Grinton in upper Swaledale.

Bodin held the manors of Grinton and Reeth in 1086, but it is not known if he built the actual fortress. What is known is that Gilbert de Gant was succeeded by his son Walter, who in 1094 inherited all the family's English lands. Walter, who eventually owned all of Swaledale through his marriage to Maud, the daughter of Count Stephen of Brittany, died about 1138–1139 and the next we hear is of a claim for half the forest of Swaledale being made in 1207–1208 against Gilbert de Gant by Brian, son of Alan, probably a Bodin heir. Despite this, the de Gant family remained in possession until they probably gave both it and the church to the Augustinians at Bridlington Priory, which was founded about 1113 by Walter de Gant. The priory held the manor of the heirs of the de Gants until 1538. Much later the Swales family appeared on the scene and having acquired Swale Hall, sought to establish its claim to the manor of West Grinton, based on the marriage of John de Swale and Alice, sister of Walter de Gant. It was held that Alice was the mother of Alured de Swaledale who in or about 1157 was granted the manor by his uncle. The Swales family lived here for

52

centuries, apparently without claiming manorial rights, until in 1578 John Swale made a settlement of the 'manor of Swale' and a watermill and lands in West Grinton. They lived in what became the family seat until 1786 when Swale Hall was sold by auction.

The site can be seen from the road on the right-hand side when you approach the village from the east. Ample parking space is available at the back of The Bridge Inn public house.

GUISBOROUGH

The ancient town of Guisborough (Ghigesburgh in the Domesday Book) is located 10 miles to the southeast of Middlesbrough, near the northern edge of the North York Moors National Park. Writing in 1607, Camden was charmed with the beauty of its position and surroundings: 'The place is really fine, and may in point of pleasantness and a graceful variety, compare with Puteoli in Italy; and in point of healthfulness, it far surpasses it. The coldness of the air which the sea occasions, is qualified and broken by the hills between; the soil is fruitful, and produces grass and fine flowers a great part of the year.' Guisborough Priory, founded in 1119 by the second Robert de Brus, Lord Skelton, was once described as 'the pride and glory of Guisborough, and one of the most wealthy, magnificent, and extensive monastic institutions in the kingdom' (Bulmer, 1890).

There is also reputed to have been a castle here, but it remains the most elusive. 'If a castle ever existed at Guisborough, certainly not the faintest trace of the earthworks which usually mark the site of a Norman stronghold are now to be found, or indeed appear to have been visible for many centuries,' wrote I'Anson. 'If, on the very scant evidence we possess, we come to the conclusion that the Earl [Robert, Earl of Mortain and of Cornwall and half-brother of William the Conqueror] did construct a fortress here, it would probably be destroyed when he rebelled in 1088, and when Rufus confiscated his Yorkshire property.' It was writer and antiquary the Reverend James Dallaway F.S.A. who in 1833 mentioned a castle as having existed here in a series of discourses on architecture in England from the Norman era to the close of the reign of Queen Elizabeth. In his work *The History and Antiquities of Cleveland* (1844–1846), historian John

Walker Ord attributes the castle to Robert de Brus and actually describes its location: the structure stood in 'the large field close to the lane going from Church Street to Redcar, called War's Field. Part of the moat may still be distinguished in this and the adjoining field, with elevated ridges and uneven surfaces, occupying several acres of ground'. But I'Anson ruled out any connection between this site and a Norman fortress: 'These earthworks, which are well known to the present writer, have certainly never had anything to do with a Norman castle; they may, perhaps, represent the one-time existence of enclosures, outbuildings, and a pond attached to the Priory Home Farm.'

Perhaps time will tell who is correct, but both Ord and I'Anson were local to the area and Ord was actually born and is buried in Guisborough. The name Wars' Fields is believed to be derived from an engagement during the English Civil War between 700 Royalist troops, under the command of Colonel Slingsby, and a large body of Roundheads, commanded by Sir Hugh Cholmley and Sir Matthew Boynton, in which the Royalists were defeated and their leader taken prisoner (Bulmer, 1890).

HELMSLEY

Perhaps one of the best known castles in this book is situated close to the beautiful Rievaulx Abbey on the southern fringe of the North York Moors. The picturesque market town of Helmsley is the natural gateway for exploring Ryedale and the surrounding moorland. More than 100 years ago I'Anson wrote, 'With its quaint houses and broad, sunny marketplace, the pleasant market town of Helmsley has an air of comfort, cleanliness and rural prosperity.' And nobody would argue with that even today. Walter Espec, builder of both the original timber structures at Rievaulx and the formidable fortress at Helmsley, no doubt chose this location for its proximity to the rich agricultural land of the Vale of Pickering and the adjacent wilderness (formerly forest but now moorland) with its ample hunting possibilities.

There has been speculation that this site was originally a prehistoric enclosure, specifically an Iron Age hill fort, or is perhaps of Roman origin. However, I'Anson attributes the earthworks to Espec in 1131

The Battle of the Standard is commemorated in this window at All Saints Parish Church, Helmsley.

and likens the fortress to a castle within a castle. There is no evidence of a motte and it is unknown whether there was a timber keep. But the two massive earthwork banks and deep ditches means there would have been strong defences in timber. The inner bailey was originally reached through the northwest entrance. Beyond this was the outer bailey that now lies under a car park. I'Anson assures us that the inner ward of the rectangular earthworks would have contained a timber great hall and solar occupying roughly the site of the stone remains visible today.

After Espec's death without issue in 1153, the fortress passed to the de Roos family through the marriage of Peter de Roos to Espec's sister, Adeline. And it is to the de Roos family that chroniclers wrongly give credit for founding the castle, as I'Anson points out: 'The erection of Helmsley Castle is always assigned to Robert de Roos, probably on the authority of Dugdale and Camden; but this would only appear to be one

An artist's impression of the first earth and timber fortress at Helmsley.

of several instances known to the writer where the honour of actually founding a certain castle is given by monastic chroniclers, to the man who first substituted masonry for timbering.' Robert de Roos indeed strengthened the timber defences in masonry some time after 1186, when the inner bank of the ringwork was levelled and replaced by a 4½m-high curtain wall with round corner towers. A new main entrance to the inner bailey was subsequently built in the southeast corner together with a new outer bailey, and many further enhancements were carried out. In the fourteenth century, Robert's son William completely remodelled the castle's defences and accommodation.

In 1478, the castle was sold to Richard, Duke of Gloucester, who was later crowned King Richard III. However, on Richard's death at the Battle of Bosworth in 1485, it reverted to the de Roos family. From 1508 until 1632 it was in the possession of the Manners family, who built a house in the shell of the west tower and twelfth-century hall. Subsequently it passed by marriage to George Villiers, 1st Duke of Buckingham and was a Royalist stronghold during the Civil War. The

Duncombe family finally bought the Helmsley estate and the fortress was abandoned when the present Duncombe Park was completed in 1713.

The photogenic All Saints Parish Church is more than worth a visit. Dedicated in 1838 and largely the result of major restoration work carried out in the Victorian era, it was built on Norman foundations and has an interesting stained-glass window commemorating the Battle of the Standard, which took place on Cowton Moor near Northallerton in 1138.

HOOD (or HOD) HILL

The remains of this former fortress are next to the Kilburn White Horse chalk figure at Sutton Bank, amid magnificent scenery on the western side of the North York Moors escarpment. Clearly these remains eluded I'Anson when he wrote in 1913, 'That the Mowbrays erected a timber castle at Hod, or Hood Grange, near Thirsk, would appear to be proved by an entry in the Close Rolls for 1218; but up to the present the writer has been unable to find the slightest trace of this fortress.' Whellan had already noted in 1859 that Hood Hill, a wooded area overlooking Hood Grange to the north, 'had the appearance of an irregularly built castle', but the mystery didn't unfold until 1970 when Whitaker suggested that Hood Hill was the actual site of the castle. It wasn't until a detailed survey by Dennison in 2000 that the series of steep slopes, banks and ditches were confirmed as early Norman and thus the true site of Hood Castle, although the suggestion that the site might have had much earlier origins lingers. 'The nature and location of the encircling ditch suggests that the monument did not originate as a small prehistoric hill-fort or enclosure, as some authors have implied, although this cannot be totally discounted at this time,' wrote Dennison in 2000.

Attributed to Robert de Stuteville (1086–1106), Lord of the Manor of Kilburn (Whitaker, 1970), the castle passed to Henry I after de Stuteville's downfall. In 1913, I'Anson wrote: 'In the *Progenies Moubraiorum* (Newburgh Priory, vi, 320), a document not earlier than the time of Henry VIII, we are told that Roger de Mowbray, son of Nigel de Albini, lived at the "castellum de Hode," to which he brought

A distant Hood Hill with Whitestone Cliff and Lake Gormire in the foreground (photograph by Dennis Bromage).

a lion from the Holy Land! William, son of Nigel de Mowbray, previous to 1222, is said to have confirmed to Byland [abbey] all donations in the vill of Angoteby subtus Hode Castrum. The one-time existence of a castle at Hode is, however, well authenticated by an entry in the Close Rolls for 1218. And in the Licences to Crenellate (Patent Rolls, 48 Henry III), permission is given to John D'Eyvill in 1257, to crenellate La Hode.' As the Close Rolls entry for 1218 mentions that the castle was 'partly in ruins and partly extant', it has been suggested that D'Eyvill (one of various spellings) was effectively building a replacement for the original timber motte and bailey castle (Whitaker, 1970).

At one stage the castle appears to have served as the stronghold of an outlaw band. 'The writer is informed by Mr. W.T. Lancaster, F.S.A., that a tradition exists to the effect that Hode was the headquarters of a notable band of robbers in the time of Edward II,' wrote I'Anson. 'Rymer tells us that "a noted robber, Sir Gosceline Deyville, who was of good family, was the leader of a band of robbers in this district in the time of Edward II, and that he attacked and rifled the Bishop's Palace at Northallerton. He was finally captured by the Sheriff and hanged at York". Stowe says, "Sir Goscelin Deivile and his brother, Robert, with 200 men in the habit of friars, did many notable robberies; they spoiled the Bishop of Durham's palaces, leaving nothing in them but bare walls." Leland who wrote at the time of Henry VIII tells us that Sir Gotselyn Daivil, a partisan of Thomas Earl of Lancaster, was finally executed for robbery.' The last-known mention of the castle is in a document dated 1322, when John de Vescy's wife, Isabella, held the castle and manor (Patent Rolls, Edward II).

The commanding position of Hood Castle is best appreciated from Roulston Scar at a point on the Cleveland Way just opposite Hood Hill. The view from the top of Sutton Bank is considered by many to be among the finest in Yorkshire. Among those who have enjoyed the extravagant vista was the Thirsk veterinary surgeon known to millions of television fans as James Herriot, who reckoned he must have stopped off there thousands of times while on his rounds (*Yorkshire Life* magazine, September 2013). Due to the precipitous nature of the ridge, the site can only be reached from either end. In fact, excavations in 2000 showed that the main approach would have been from the north, where a separate barbican probably stood. Accessibility was greatly enhanced in 2009 by the laying of a path across the castle mound and down the northern slope. For the more energetic, a circular walk (8.25km) starts at the National Park Visitor Centre at Sutton Bank and descends via Thieves Highway, returning via the White Horse hill figure.

HUNMANBY

The bustling village of Hunmanby lies on the northeastern edge of the Wolds escarpment, 3 miles southwest of the coastal resort of Filey. Claimed to once have been the largest village in the country, its name dates back to the time when wolves were hunted on the Wolds and the Danes area was in occupation (Hundemanbi in the Domesday Book or 'farmstead of the houndsmen'). Indeed, King Stephen reputedly kept wolfhounds here and the manor once ranked among the most important in the north of England. The motte and bailey castle that

Castlegarth in Hunmanby: a motte and bailey fortress once stood here.

once existed in Hunmanby is attributed to Guilbert de Gant (1048–1095), the first Norman lord of the manor and nephew of William the Conqueror. Destroyed by William le Gros about 1143–1144 during the civil war in the reign of King Stephen, the remains are in a wooded area to the west of the village, which is skirted by the main road to Malton. Originally known as 'Castlegarth', the site was included in the parkland of Hunmanby Hall during the eighteenth century. Known today as Castle Hill, the earthworks occupy the highest point on a natural knoll and comprise a motte bounded by a steep road embankment to the north and a partially infilled ditch. The bailey has been much altered by terracing associated with modern buildings, but the northern area remains undeveloped and is estimated to be a quarter of the original area. Formerly a private school for girls, the adjacent Hunmanby Hall was redeveloped into luxury flats in 1991 and the park turned into a private golf course. Nearby All Saints Church dates from the late eleventh or early twelfth centuries, but there was almost certainly a Saxon church here before that time. Local finds, such as Roman pottery, flint axe and arrowheads, and a British chariot burial from the first or second century BC, have been recorded in the area, showing that Hunmanby was occupied long before the Danes or Normans arrived.

HUTTON CONYERS

The small village of Hutton Conyers lies close to the River Ure and is just a mile northeast of the ancient cathedral city of Ripon. Several notable families have owned the land here: the Conyers, the Mallories of Studley, the Aislabies, the Earl de Grey and in the late nineteenth century, the Marquis of Ripon (Bulmer, 1890). Built about 1136–1140, the castle at Hutton Conyers is attributed to Alan Niger, Earl of Richmond, who was one of the most powerful supporters of King Stephen against the Empress Matilda. He erected it allegedly with a view to exploiting the local populace. This is supported by chronicler John of Hexam (c.1160–1209), who wrote, 'The Earl took advantage of the terrible anarchy which prevailed during the civil wars to erect the castle of Hutton Conyers for the sole purpose of exacting tribute from the inhabitants of the city of Ripon and of maltreating and extorting ransom from any persons who were unfortunate enough to fall into the clutches of the garrison of the fortress.' The earl got his comeuppance on or about 1154 when order was restored and the robber den was dismantled and destroyed by order of Henry II.

The earthworks at Hutton Conyers, as viewed from a main-street garden.

61

A photograph showing that the Hutton Conyers site was once used as a motocross track.

I'Anson noted that this fate had also befallen the fortress at Yafforth and suggested that the people of Ripon themselves might actually have been responsible for destroying the earthworks, which in his day were already mutilated to an extent that made it impossible to visualise the original design. He estimated that the castle comprised a square central platform (as at Helmsley) defended by outworks and a series of concentric ditches and banks. Sadly, details recorded even a century ago were few, but I'Anson imagined there were two oblong courts on the north and east, and he also saw traces of an ancient road leading to the entrance at the southeast angle of the eastern enclosure. The castle site shares a field immediately to the north of the village main street with the earthworks of an old moated manor house of a later date attributed to the Conyers family. A sixteenth-century farmhouse occupied the site until as recently as 1869 and featured a ceiling ornamented with the arms of the Mallory family, who were the lords of the manor when it was built. But the Conyers family, from whom the village takes its name, were associated with the village since the late eleventh century. The estate was divided at the end of the twelfth century and when the last Conyers male heir died some time after 1334, the estate passed by marriage to Sir Christopher Mallory. It remained in the Mallory family until 1670 when the manor passed by marriage to George Aislabie and subsequently to his descendants. In 1845 the estates reverted to descendants of two female members of the Aislabie and Mallory families, through which it passed to the Earl de Grey and ultimately to the Marquess of Ripon (Page, 1914).

KILDALE

The village of Kildale lies at the northern extremity of the Cleveland Hills, approximately 3 miles southeast of Great Ayton and within the North York Moors National Park. The Cleveland Way National Trail runs through the village, which is the site of the former Percy stronghold known as 'Hall Garth' and is in very pleasant surroundings close to the Church of St Cuthbert. 'Charmingly situated in a narrow secluded and beautiful moorland vale, snugly tucked away between the towering heights of Percy Cross and Kempwithen, not far from the source of the River Leven,' wrote I'Anson. More than a century ago, he described the earthwork as 'very much silted down and defaced', not least due to a railway cutting that slices through the motte. He imagined it had probably been deliberately lowered at some time, as was the case at Whorlton, and found no trace of a bailey, although it was suggested to him that the adjacent churchyard might hold a clue. 'Mrs Armitage says, in a letter to the writer, "An old man whom I met there in 1902 said he has always been told the castle stood on the rising ground west of the church, at the east end of the knoll. He also said there used to be a well there, but that it dried up when the railway cutting was made. There is now a farmhouse and a clump of trees on the knoll. The ground falls all round, probably marking the site of a ditch." This ditch may be clearly traced on the north and north-west sides of the motte, and is marked on the six-inch ordnance map as "remains of moat." Mrs Armitage adds: "I strongly suspect that the churchyard was formerly the bailey; it has something like a ditch on the east side, and on the north-west I saw something like the fragment of a bank."'

The earthworks at Kildale viewed from St Cuthbert's churchyard.

A railway cutting on the Esk valley line slices through the motte at Kildale.

There are several ancient references to a 'castle' having existed on the site and I'Anson suggested it might have been founded early in the reign of Stephen and probably developed into a stone fortress, more along the lines of a fortified manor house than a feudal castle. The Percys of Kildale held sway here for many generations and when John de Percy died towards the close of the fifteenth century, the property passed to Lord Henry Percy. By 1508 the manor had been sold to the earls of Northumberland, who held it until the reign of Charles I. It was subsequently abandoned when nearby Kildale Hall was built in the nineteenth century.

The site, which is on private land, is most conveniently viewed from the churchyard of St Cuthbert's, which is reached via a narrow footbridge that crosses the railway line. Although the current church only dates from 1868, it was built with typical Victorian fantasy in a thirteenth-century style. The entrance porch, for which the oldest stones were reused, is adorned with sculptures presumably representing former members of the Percy family, whose coat of arms is evident on a number of grave slabs.

The porch of St Cuthbert's Church, Kildale, has this interesting effigy harking back to the medieval period.

KILLERBY

Known locally as 'Castle Hills', the remains of this fortress are situated in a bend of the River Swale, between Catterick and the village of Killerby on land that was formerly a swamp. The location was strategically important as the castle was close to two main Roman roads leading to Catterick (Caractonium) and it also commanded a ford on the Swale. Probably built by Scolland, a senior servant to Count Alan of Richmond, about 1120–1125, the castle passed by marriage to the FitzBrian family in whose possession it remained until being abandoned in 1291. The last occupant, Brian FitzAlan, erected a stone castle nearby. I'Anson wrote, 'An excellent history of this distinguished soldier is contained in The Early History of Bedale. The Fitz-Alans of Killerby Castle must not be confused with their namesakes, the Fitz-Alans, Earls of Arundel, with whom they were not connected in any way. Brian Fitz-Alan died in 1306. His singularly beautiful effigy still remains in Bedale Church. A local tradition exists that Brian Fitz-Alan also erected a castle at Bedale, but there is not a shred of evidence to support it, and it is most improbable that he built two stone castles so close together.'

The appearance of impregnability particularly caught I'Anson's eye: 'It stands at the northern end of the earthworks, surrounded by a ditch, which completely isolates it from the bailey. The latter is still in fair preservation. On the east its ramparts rise to a height of no less than 60 feet above the swamps of the River Swale and are very formidable in appearance. It is quite possible, previous to a great flood in 1771, that the river may have washed the base of this side of the bailey.' The corners of the ramparts were well preserved when I'Anson visited the site 100 years ago and he believed they once carried small timber towers. He further suggested that the motte would have been a citadel pure and simple, with access to the summit gained from the bailey via a bridge or ladder that could be drawn up onto the top of the motte when desired, as at Topcliffe. 'One is inclined to think that the timber great hall, solar, kitchen, etc. always stood within the bailey.'

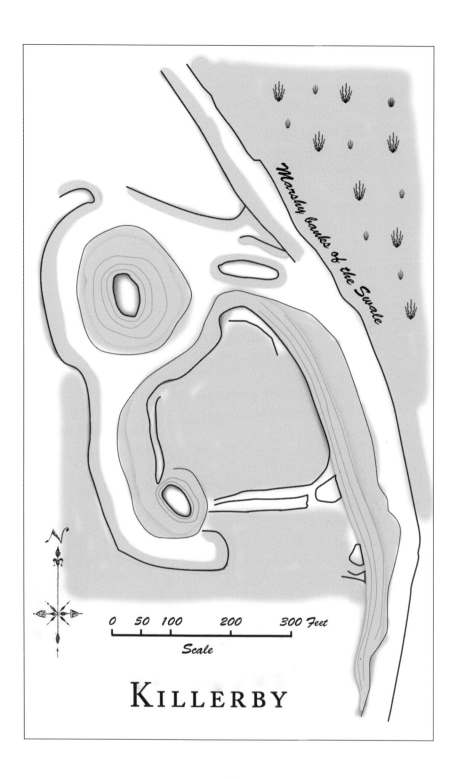

Marshy banks of the Swale

0   50 100   200   300 Feet
Scale

KILLERBY

KILTON

Perched high above Kilton Beck, just over 3 miles from Skelton Castle and 5 miles from Guisborough Priory, Kilton Castle is thought to have been founded by Pagan – a feudatory of the Percy family of Topcliffe – during the reign of Stephen (I'Anson). Dating from between 1135 and 1140, the timber castle was rebuilt in stone by the de Kylton family between 1190 and 1200. By 1222 the castle had passed by marriage to Robert de Thweng, who found himself caught up in a dispute with the prior of Guisborough concerning a matter that arose during the infirmity of his wife's uncle, Sir William de Kylton. In a nutshell, de Kylton held the right to appoint a priest to the wealthy church at Kirkleatham. The prior, however, took advantage of Sir William during an illness when he appeared to be on his deathbed and persuaded him to bequeath the church and thus relinquish his right to appoint a priest. Sir William recovered and sought to reverse the alleged 'gift', but the dispute was still raging when Robert, the grandson of one of the most powerful lords of Yorkshire, inherited his grandfather's extensive lands and made Kilton Castle the caput of the family estate. Frustrated by the lack of progress in dealing with his grievance and being the character he was, Robert took the law into his own hands. Using the pseudonym 'Will Wither' – meaning 'William the Angry' – he sought justice by raiding church properties and distributing the spoils to the poor. This rash action backfired and resulted in his temporary excommunication, but thanks to the support of many powerful northern families, not to mention Henry III, who made representations to Pope Gregory IX on his behalf, he was officially pardoned. In 1229 the Kirkleatham issue was resolved in Robert's favour and in 1240 he went on crusade with Richard, 1st Earl of Cornwall and younger brother of Henry III, but there is doubt as to whether or not he ever reached the Holy Land. He is thought to have died by 1257, the year in which his son Marmaduke was apparently in control of the major Thweng estates.

The castle ruins at Kilton occupy the summit of a promontory not unlike the site of the former stronghold at Mount Ferrant, but are even more defensible thanks to the steep-to-sheer slopes surrounding the site. All that was needed to isolate the natural motte was a ditch cut across the promontory into the ravines on both sides. Originally built in timber between 1135 and 1140, the stronghold was developed in masonry between 1190 and 1200, but was described as 'small and worthless' between 1341 and 1345. It was totally abandoned during the sixteenth century. The ruins are at the end of a farm track that joins the road halfway between Kilton and Kilton Thorpe, but are on private land and viewing requires permission from the Skelton Estate Office in Saltburn.

KIPPAX

Kippax (pronounced Kippis or Kippish locally) is a village lying 8 miles east of Leeds and 6 miles northwest of Pontefract. It was an important place as far back as the late Anglo-Saxon period and during the early Norman period, when it was the administrative centre for the honour of Pontefract. Held by Ilbert de Lacy, to whom the castle is attributed, the honour subsequently moved its headquarters to Barwick-in-Elmet and by the late twelfth century Kippax had lost its strategic importance. Known locally as 'Cheney Basin', the castle site lies close to the centre of the village on Manor Garth Hill, immediately north of the eleventh-century Church of St Mary. Standing on the brow of a hill, the church is a prominent feature of the landscape and is difficult to miss. The earthwork comprises a circular enclosure or ringwork with a partially surrounding ditch. Traces of a wall still exist to the southeast and to the west the church hall is thought to stand upon further defensive features. If there ever was a bailey it was likely located in the area now occupied by the churchyard. The site never developed beyond earth and timber defences due to the previously mentioned decline in the status of Kippax. A medieval document dated 1322 refers to the site's value as a herb garden, which suggests that the castle was probably dismantled by that date. Today it is grassed over and is a feature for the general public to enjoy. There is no record of excavations on the site, but a recent geophysical survey failed to define any structures that might still lie buried.

The unusual name Kippax is of Anglo-Saxon origin and first appeared as Chipesch in the Domesday Book and as 'Kippeys' in charters from the 1090s to the 1270s. From the thirteenth century onwards it appeared as Kypask and Kypax. The name's origin is thought to be a composition of an Anglo-Saxon personal name, Cippa or Cyppa, combined with *æsc* (meaning 'ash tree'), suggesting that the village was first established in an area populated by ash trees. By the time of the Domesday Book Kippax was the centre of a large estate that stretched northwards from the River Aire as far as Aberford. A church at Kippax is mentioned in the Domesday Book and in the 1870s a Roman coffin was found beneath the nave of St Mary's Church during its restoration. A few years later fragments of an Anglian cross-shaft were discovered built into a doorway in the west wall of the tower. Now preserved in the nave, the stone was dated about AD 900. Further finds near the church included a Neolithic stone axe that is now deposited with Leeds Museum.

KIRKBY FLEETHAM

Once two distinct villages, Kirkby Fleetham is pleasantly situated approximately 5 miles west of Northallerton. The motte and bailey fortress once stood on a natural rise in a low-lying area to the south of the village and is attributed to Henry le Scrope, who bought the manor at Fleetham in 1301. At some point after his death in 1336 the family abandoned the site as their principal residence and later in the century Henry's son Richard, 1st Lord Scrope of Bolton built the magnificent stone edifice at Castle Bolton near Wensleydale. The family held land in Fleetham until 1628 and it was through this line that the manor eventually passed to Lord Fauconberg and the Darcy family.

Kirkby's name is derived from the Old Norse for 'village with a church'. After the Norman Conquest the land belonged to Count Alan of Brittany, but after 1086 it was granted to Odo, chamberlain to the Earl of Richmond. Gospatrick, son of Aldred (Eldred), held Kirkby manor and was succeeded by his daughter Godareda. From this point the succession is uncertain until William Giffard emerged in the thirteenth century. He was succeeded by the Stapleton and Metham families in that order. The two manors were finally united in 1670 when the title of Fleetham was conveyed to Richard Smelt, a younger brother of the lord of Kirkby. In 1740 the Aislabie family and subsequently the Courage family succeeded to the title.

Kirkby Fleetham's motte and bailey fortress was once surrounded by marshland.

It is easy to imagine the fortress being surrounded by marshland when it was built in the early fourteenth century. A depression on the western side of the motte might have originally held water, and indeed the entire area surrounding the site was probably waterlogged. The bailey would have occupied the raised area to the southeast of the motte. To the south of this is thought to have been a defensive ditch that drained into Mill Beck. A depression to the east of the bailey might have been a fishpond, and to the north and along the road in a southerly direction are features relating to medieval dwellings.

KIRKBY MALZEARD

The unspoilt village of Kirkby Malzeard lies 7 miles northwest of Ripon amid charming countryside. The well-preserved motte and bailey earthwork is at the northeastern extremity of the village on private ground in a heavily wooded area overlooking Kex Beck. First mentioned in 1131, it was one of three Mowbray castles slighted after the insurrection in 1173–1174 after being besieged and captured when

Roger de Mowbray joined a conspiracy to replace the king with his cousin. Although he surrendered and received a pardon from Henry II, his castles at Thirsk and Kirkby were demolished in 1176. The Mowbrays remained lords of Kirkby until the late fifteenth century when Anne, the only daughter of John Mowbray, 4th Duke of Norfolk, died without issue. The association between Kirkby and the Mowbray family finally ended in 1490 when Thomas Stanley, Earl of Derby, acquired the manor. His descendants held it until the eighteenth century.

The motte, which survived landscaping carried out in the nineteenth century, is relatively low, but the steeply declining land to the west gave it natural protection. There is more of a gradual descent to the large bailey, which projects beyond the wooded area into pastureland to the south and is separated from it by a public road. There are signs of a rampart and ditch, and excavations have shown that stone defences once existed.

KIRKBYMOORSIDE

The small but ancient market town of Kirkbymoorside is very pleasantly situated on the southern edge of the North York Moors, roughly halfway between Pickering and Helmsley. The moors escarpment rises above it to the north and east; to the south, two moorland streams, Hodge Beck and the River Dove, flow into Ryedale where countless acres of fertile meadowland stretch towards the distant Wolds. Overlooking the town and just a short walk from the church is Vivers Hill, from the summit of which distant views can be had to the south and landmarks, such as Oliver's Mount near Scarborough, are visible to the east on a clear day. Immediately to the north lies the beautiful scenery of the North York Moors, including the quaint village of Hutton-le-Hole, home to Ryedale Folk Museum. Kirkbymoorside itself is rich in history: ancient British, Viking and Anglo-Saxon remains have been found in the area and the town once had two baronial residences, a medieval castle and a fortified manor house, which caught Whellan's attention in the mid-eighteenth century. 'One is the moated site of a castle, on the east side of the town, in an elevated situation, which belonged to the Stuteville family. The site of the other castle, which is known as Manor Garth, is at the north end of the street called Castle Gate. This was occasionally the residence of the Nevilles, whose chief seat was Raby Castle in the county of Durham. A small portion of the outer wall of the latter building remains to this day.' By following Castle Gate to the end and turning left at Castle Lodge, visitors will see the small section of wall mentioned above: it lies straight ahead just beyond the gate. The site of the former moated castle on Vivers Hill is to the east of the marketplace behind the Church of All Saints. Follow the churchyard footpath uphill and go into the field beyond the kissing gate. The site is among the trees beyond the pond. The earthworks comprise a well-defined moat enclosing a raised and terraced area of approximately 90 x 70m. Other features within this area are thought to be traces of former buildings. There is an outstanding view to the south, although this is now somewhat impeded by tree growth.

The earth and timber castle is attributed to Robert de Stuteville, in whose day the Kirkbymoorside estate, which included Farndale, Bransdale and Gillamoor, would have been excellent hunting country. Roger de Mowbray held the manor in the reign of Henry II (1154–1189), when Robert III de Stuteville laid claim to the estate. A settlement of ten knights' fees was agreed, but not having received a royal stamp of approval, the settlement was later challenged in a dispute between William de Stuteville, son of Robert, and William de Mowbray, grandson of Roger. It ended with the de Stuteville heirs holding the manor until it came into the possession of the Crown at the end of the fourteenth century. In 1859 Whellan wrote, 'King Henry I deprived the heads of the houses of Mowbray and Stuteville of their possessions on account of their rebellion and bestowed the greater part of them on Nigel de Albini, a young Norman nobleman, who married the heiress of the Mowbrays and by command of the King assumed the name of Mowbray. He continued to hold the estates of the Stutevilles till the time of Henry II, when the above mentioned dispute arose between the Mowbrays and the Stutevilles; the last of which families was again restored to favour, and the barony of Kirbymoorside given to them.'

In the thirteenth century the Wake family came into possession of the estates following the marriage of Joan de Stuteville to Hugh de Wake. It was Joan who originated the custom for women to ride sidesaddle, which historians wrongly ascribe to Queen Anne, wife of Richard II and daughter of the Emperor Wenceslaus. Her seal depicted a woman riding sidesaddle (*Historia Rievallencis*). The Wake family inheritance was ultimately shared by three co-heiresses, one of whom married the earl of Westmorland who succeeded to the barony. But the castle was abandoned by the mid-fourteenth century after the plague had taken its toll in Kirkbymoorside. In 1408 ownership passed to the Neville family who built the nearby hunting lodge known as Neville Castle. This is believed to have replaced the earlier site on Vivers Hill as the main seat of the manor of Kirkbymoorside. The Neville family held it from the beginning of the fifteenth century until 1569, when it once again forfeited to the Crown following the rebellion of Charles Neville, 6th Earl of Westmorland.

While in Kirkbymoorside, it is worth visiting St Gregory's Minster at the bottom of the quiet and secluded Kirkdale. There was a church in this delightfully shady spot even before Anglo-Saxon times and excavations suggest it might have once been a pagan site. The inscription on the sundial mounted over the south door is considered the oldest example of an Anglo-Saxon carving ever found.

LAUGHTON-EN-LE-MORTHEN

Laughton-en-le-Morthen is a small village of great antiquity that lies to the southeast of Rotherham and is known to have been of considerable importance in Saxon times, possibly even the site of a Brigantian stronghold. Situated in a well-wooded area to the southwest of Tickhill, it has a fine, fourteenth-century parish church (All Saints), the spire of which is visible for miles around. The well-preserved motte and bailey earthworks are next to the church and the churchyard actually occupies what used to be the outer bailey. At the time of the Norman Conquest this historic village was the location of a hall owned by Earl Edwin of Mercia, brother-in-law of Earl Harold who became king of England. But in 1086 the manor was in the hands of Roger de Busli, the castle's founder, as part of the honour of Tickhill. Upon the death of Roger's son, the honour was given to Robert de Belesme, Earl of Shrewsbury, whose estates were eventually seized by Henry I. Henry died in 1135, but the honour of Tickhill remained with the Crown until Prince Edward, son of Henry III, gave it to Geoffrey de Lusignan. By the reign of Edward II (1307–1327), Drogo de Merlawe was lord of the manor and in 1332 the lordship had passed by marriage to Ralph, Earl of Eu. In 1369–1370, Robert, Earl of Eu held the manor, but his English lands were seized by the Crown for his allegiance to the king of France during the Hundred Years War. Edward III subsequently granted the manor to John of Gaunt, whose son, Henry IV, succeeded to the title. A sick man towards the end of his reign and probably suffering from leprosy, Henry had once dreamed of going on a crusade. Fittingly he died in the 'Jerusalem' Chamber at the house of the Abbot of Westminster in 1413.

LOCKINGTON

Lockington is a small village situated roughly halfway between Beverley and Driffield in pleasant undulating countryside on the fringe of the Yorkshire Wolds. It is the location of a former motte and bailey castle, probably built by Nigel Fossard, on a site known as Coney Hills, which is on private property close to Hall Garth Farm off Bealey's Lane. A copse of ancient trees marking the site can be seen by looking south from the car park of the Church of St Mary. Little is known about the history of the castle other than the fact that members of the Fossard family were lords of the manor here from 1071. Nigel's grandson William, who died in 1169, built the first church at Lockington about 1150 and his manor house was located at the hamlet of Barf Hill, just 3 miles east of Lockington. The castle is thought to have been abandoned in the late thirteenth century when a new, moated hall was built in the castle bailey to the east of the motte. This later moated site was itself abandoned when a new building, Hall Garth, was built in 1685. Measuring roughly 50m across, the motte rises 4m above the encircling ditch with the bailey to the east. In 1913, I'Anson wrote: 'The motte and bailey castle of Lockington, which was always a favourite residence of the Fossards and of their successors, the Mauleys, is still in very fair preservation. The motte is only 14 feet high, and that it never was much higher is shown by the fact that it

The distant copse marks the site known as Coney Hills where the Fossards built a motte and bailey castle.

still retains a portion of its banquette. The bailey was walled round either by Robert de Turnham or by his successor, Peter de Mauley I.' The de Mauleys, who were lords of the manor here, as well as at Mulgrave Castle, Swaledale and Doncaster, added the original south chapel of St Mary's between 1330 and 1340. Take time to look around this curious little church while you are in Lockington.

MALTON

Situated on the banks of the River Derwent, midway between York and Pickering, the bustling market town of Malton was important as early as Roman times when a fort (Deventio Brigantum) existed here from AD 71. The Normans also built a fortress in Malton, but little trace of it remains today. The motte and bailey castle might have occupied the earthworks of the Roman fort and would have dominated the river crossing and the land all around. In the early twelfth century, a new stone castle was built, the only known illustration of which is on a map dated 1399 in the British Library, which shows a substantial round tower. In the sixteenth century, Leland described the ruined stone castle as having been large.

I'Anson assigned the original motte and bailey castle to Eustace FitzJohn, a close friend of Henry I and founder of the Priory of St Mary in 1150. Eustace had gained the castles and estates of Alnwick and Malton through marriage to Beatrice de Vescy, which made him powerful in the region. But the English monarchy was uncomfortable with the family's closeness to the Scottish royal family and in 1138, after Eustace had supported King David by marching with the Scottish army into Yorkshire, King Stephen laid siege to the castle for eight days during his wars with Matilda. The Scots and their supporters were defeated at the Battle of the Standard (also known as the Battle of Northallerton) in 1138. Upon the death of Eustace in 1157, his son William succeeded and assumed his mother's family name of de Vesci. William was succeeded in turn by his son Eustace, and one of these two were responsible for reinforcing the fortress with works in masonry. This is likely to have taken place before 1194, the year that Richard the Lionheart and the king of Scotland met in Malton. King John ordered the fortress to be dismantled in 1213 following the submission of the barons and this was only reprieved by the king's death in 1216. When William de Vescy was killed at Bannockburn in 1314 without an heir, the castle reverted to the Crown. In 1317 it was granted to John de Mowbray, who was bizarrely refused admission. In 1322 Robert de Brus seized the castle after the defeat of Edward II, but he decided to destroy it before retreating northwards later that year.

In 1387 the castle passed by marriage to Sir Ralph Eure. This ancient Yorkshire family defended Scarborough Castle against the Pilgrimage of Grace in 1536 and became wardens of the East Marches. They held the castle for the next few centuries, but at the time of Leland's *Itinerary* (1535–1543) it was described as being in ruins and as only having 'a mean house for a farmer' standing on the site. During the English Civil War, Malton was under siege again and Newcastle's forces were defeated here by Sir William Constable. In 1604, Ralph,

Lord Eure built a spectacular mansion on the site, of which only the lodge remains. The house was demolished in 1674 and the stones were literally divided between two sisters who had quarrelled for 20 years over their inheritance. The Old Lodge Hotel is the remaining fragment of the original Jacobean mansion and its size hints at the former grandeur of the mansion, which was by all accounts of royal proportions. The Old Lodge is in Old Maltongate at the northern extremity of the town on the east side of the main road leading to Pickering and Whitby. More than 100 years ago I'Anson wrote, 'The site of the castle is in the grounds of "The Lodge" [now Castle Garden] – the residence of the Hon. Geoffrey Dawnay, to whom the writer is indebted for showing him around. It was admirably situated for defensive purposes, being placed at the angle of a promontory, but all that now remains is an angular fragment of the earthen rampart. No trace of a motte remains.'

In 1995, Ryedale District Council acquired 5 acres of land behind the Old Lodge Hotel in Old Maltongate with 2,000 years of history buried beneath its soil. Today the Malton Castle Garden is open to the general public and can be accessed either via a doorway in the wall along Castlegate, or the main entrance at Orchard Fields, which can be reached via Old Maltongate and Sheepfoot Hill. 'Malton Castle played an important part in English history locally and nationally. Today all that remains is a street name and a few remnants of wall,' explains the Castle Garden website, which rather uniquely has a link to a video clip showing the site being excavated in the mid-1990s. Five trenches were dug, but only the seventeenth-century mansion was located. The precise location of the medieval castle remains elusive; however, a medieval curtain wall has been identified in a garden backing onto Castlegate and it would be a fair assumption that the Norman stronghold would have stood at the extreme end of the wooded high ground that falls steeply away at the town end of the garden.

MEXBOROUGH

Located 8 miles southwest of Doncaster at the northeastern end of a dyke known as the Roman Ridge, Mexborough (Mechesburg in the Domesday Book) is a small yet ancient market town whose name alone suggests it was once fortified (burh meaning a fortified place in Old English). A motte and bailey castle was built here to command an ancient ford called Strafford Sands, which formed where the River Dearne flows into the River Don. The castle is attributed to Roger de Busli, who held the nearby honour of Tickhill. Writing in the seventeenth century, English antiquary Roger Dodsworth said, 'Mexborough, where hath once been a castle', suggesting that stone ruins had been visible on the motte. However, at least one other source suggests that the castle was never developed in stone (Hey, 2003).

The remains of the fortress are in Castle Park, a wooded area encircled by houses in the south of the town and which is open to the public during daylight hours. The entrance to the circular bailey is from the northwest where there is an unusual and additional crescent-shaped bank and ditch that might have served as an extra defence, much like a barbican. There are no clear signs of an outer bailey, but traces of banking and ditching on the west side of the site hint at there once having been a protected court on that side (Chalkley Gould, 1904).

Roger de Busli, a favourite of Duke William, was given lands in several counties following the Conquest and by the time of the Domesday Book he held 86 manors in Nottinghamshire and 46 in Yorkshire, in addition to others in Derbyshire, Lincolnshire, Leicestershire and Devon. He died in about 1099 without an heir and his lands passed to Robert Belleme, who forfeited them in 1102 following his part in a rebellion against Henry I. The honour of Tickhill was later given to the count of Eu.

MIDDLEHAM

Dominating the old-world market town of Middleham in Wensleydale is the magnificent stone edifice that was once the seat of powerful fifteenth-century lords. The late Norman castle, which was the childhood home of Richard III, is the main focus for visitors, but visible a mere 500yd to the south is the earthwork of the original FitzRandolph fortress, which predates the stone castle by about a century. Occupying roughly an acre, the site known as William's Hill affords fine views of both Middleham and Wensleydale. 'The view

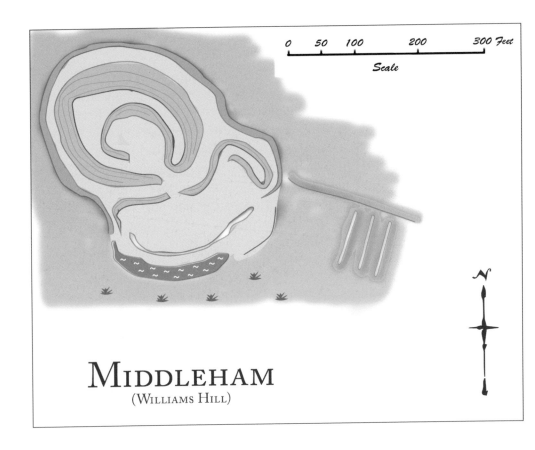

MIDDLEHAM
(WILLIAMS HILL)

from the site is beautiful,' wrote I'Anson more than 100 years ago. 'To the left the lovely Vale of Wensley winds upwards to meet the mountains of the west; just below is feudal Middleham, the Windsor of the North, the grandest of our Yorkshire castles; northward stretches a delightful and well-wooded countryside studded with villages and churches.'

Built by Ribald, the brother of Alan le Roux of Richmond and son of Count Eudo of Penthievre in Brittany, the earth and timber fortress at Middleham was erected early in the reign of Rufus (1087–1100) to defend Coverdale. When Ribald retired to become a monk at St Mary's Abbey in York, his eldest son, Ralph, inherited the fortress, which subsequently passed to Ribald's eldest grandson, Robert, who abandoned it in about 1190 in favour of the new castle. During its 100 years of occupation, the fortress would have had formidable defences and I'Anson was in no doubt that the roughly triangular platform on

William's Hill is surrounded by grazing land and is visible from Middleham Castle.

the western edge of the motte would have borne a wooden tower or keep. He also proposed that the dwelling accommodation was confined to the motte and that a great hall might have occupied the small sunken court. The entrance to the bailey on the southeastern side was still traceable in his day and would have been protected by a timber outwork.

MIRFIELD

Mirfield (Mirefelt in the Domesday Book) is a small town within the Metropolitan Borough of Kirklees in West Yorkshire and lies on the River Calder, midway between Brighouse and Dewsbury. The well-preserved Castle Hall Hill in the grounds of the thirteenth-century St Mary's Church is the site of a motte and bailey castle built between 1086 and 1159 by either Svein, son of Alric, or possibly his son, Adam, to oversee the estates of the honour of Pontefract. Mirfield and Hopton were among 214 manors bestowed upon Ilbert de Lacy after the Norman Conquest. The motte and ditch at Mirfield have survived the centuries intact and are now surrounded by urban development. The bailey, which is to the east of the motte, is occupied by the church and churchyard and was linked to the motte by a causeway. Precious little is known about the castle except that after Adam's death it was reduced in status. Following a storm in 2008 during which the church wall was blown down, the site was exposed to public view and triggered public interest that led to the removal of trees from the earthworks and a general restoration of the site.

Those interested in the legend of Robin Hood might be aware that his alleged final resting place is in nearby Kirklees Park, a mere stone's throw away from what remains of Kirklees Priory. The traditional story is that he died there after being mortally wounded, but there is also a conspiracy theory involving the prioress, under whose watchful eye his health worsened. The priory church and other buildings were demolished in 1538 and the stone used to build Kirklees Hall, which stands on the same site. The remaining priory gatehouse and Robin's tomb, appropriately located in a leafy glade, are on the private Kirklees estate and unfortunately not open for public viewing.

MOUNT FERRANT

Pleasantly situated near the village of Birdsall on the edge of the Yorkshire Wolds escarpment, the site of the former motte and bailey fortress of Mount Ferrant occupies a strategic point overlooking an old Roman road to Malton. The motte is very much silted down, but is unusually located some distance from the nab end of the promontory on which it stands, rather than at the very end. This made it necessary to dig ditches on either side to strengthen its defensive position. Three baileys are positioned to the east of the motte where the final outer bailey defences are incorporated in a field boundary.

The fortress is attributed to Nigel Fossard, a major tenant of Robert, Count of Mortain. After the death of the Conqueror in 1088, the count's lands were forfeited and passed to Fossard, who built a timber fortress on the promontory. After Fossard's death in 1120, his son, Robert, succeeded him, but difficulties with his inheritance placed the Fossard estate in the king's hands and it was only regained upon payment of a fine. Mount Ferrant was dealt a final blow in 1173–1174 when Henry II ordered its destruction as a reprisal for the Fossards' support of the Mortain Rebellion. The timbers were salvaged and used in the building of Meaux Abbey near Beverley, which was itself dismantled in 1539 and the stone used to build the defences of Kingston Upon Hull.

Only a stone's throw away from this site is what is thought might be an unfinished motte. The barely visible remains are located a few hundred metres southwest of the parish church at nearby Acklam. Little is known about this site, but there are similarly silted-down castle remains recorded on the 1in Ordnance Survey map at nearby Leppington and one is inclined to speculate that these probable motte sites were early attempts by the Fossard family at establishing a safe haven before settling at Mount Ferrant. Incidentally, Leavening Brow offers fine views to the northwest and Derwent valley, and the summit of Acklam Wold is the location of a Bronze Age round-barrow cemetery, although this has now been greatly eroded.

NORTHALLERTON

Situated in the Vale of Mowbray amid rich farmland, the ancient and bustling market town of Northallerton has traces of two former motte and bailey castles within a stone's throw of each other. The first site is at 'Castle Hills' and was probably founded by the Conqueror himself when he camped at Northallerton in 1068. In 1087 or later, Rufus gave the lordship to the bishopric of Durham, but in 1141 both Northallerton and Durham castles were seized in the name of King David of Scotland with a view to extending the Scottish border. Attack followed attack and in 1153 the castle came into the hands of Hugh de Puiset, who supported the rebel cause despite being a cousin of Henry II. He eventually surrendered his castles in 1174 and Northallerton Castle was dismantled that same year by order of Henry II.

When he visited it more than a century ago, I'Anson was somewhat harsh in his description of the town: 'Northallerton, the official capital of the North Riding, is a sleepy, old-fashioned town, possessing no objects of interest beyond the church and the site of the Bishops' Palace, and consisting of one long, wide street with broad cobbled pavements, lined with dull old houses. The antiquary who expects to find the enormous motte and the mighty earthworks of the Norman castle of the Prince-Bishops will be disappointed. All that now remains

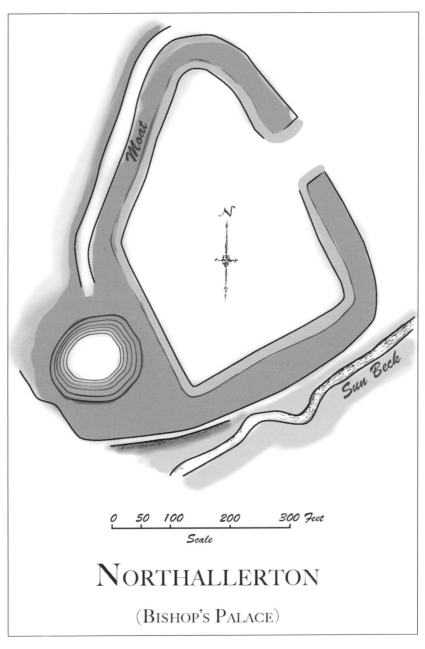

Moat

Sun Beck

0   50   100   200   300 Feet

Scale

NORTHALLERTON

(Bishop's Palace)

to mark its site is a fragment of what was the eastern rampart of the bailey, for the North Eastern Railway has put a finishing touch to the work of destruction commenced by Henry II.' I'Anson was, however, taken by the view: 'The fortress stood on relatively elevated ground with a wide and extensive view for miles over the low-lying ground, with on one side the Hambleton and on the other side the Richmondshire hills, blue and hazy in the distance.'

In the mid-nineteenth century, Ingledew described even earlier willful damage to the site when he wrote, 'About the beginning of the present century, the high embankments and trenches on the east side were taken down and leveled. After the death of Miss Lampton, the north side of the Castle Hill, which was entire, was brought down by Mr. Thomas Hunter, who took down the high mounds, which were very formidable, and filled up the deep trenches, and afterwards the north terrace, which with the rampart or terrace on the east side [still remaining], formed a kind of crescent or half circle. A strong pavement of stones, about two feet below the surface and three or four courses deep, firmly set in lime, was removed, several score loads being sold to the overseers of the highways.' The next blow to the site was dealt by the arrival of the Steam Age, as I'Anson recounts: 'In 1838 the remainder of the earthworks – with the exception of the fragment of the eastern rampart, still remaining – were leveled on the construction of the Great North of England [now North Eastern] Railway.'

The second castle at Northallerton was built in the last decade of the twelfth century. 'The origin of this castle is uncertain, but it would appear exceedingly probable that in order to raise money for the Crusade, Richard I sold to the Bishops of Durham the right to build a second castle at Northallerton,' wrote I'Anson. He reasoned that the right to build was probably sold to Hugh de Puiset when he bought the earldom of Northumberland in 1189 and that the new castle was probably finished before 1195. 'Evidently Puiset was not permitted to refortify the formidable earthworks, which marked the site of the stronghold of his predecessors. This, one imagines, would certainly have been done had not such an act been expressly forbidden – and it would therefore have been necessary to build an entirely new residence.'

The earthworks, which stand on the banks of the Sun Beck about 200yd from the church, were considered by I'Anson more in keeping with a manor house than a castle. 'When the castle developed works in masonry is unknown, but the stockading of the motte would not appear to have ever been replaced by stonework and there is no doubt that the building developed more on the lines of a moated manor-house than on those of a feudal castle, and that the motte was lowered, and abandoned as part of the edifice. Indeed, if we eliminate the motte – which may have been abandoned at a comparatively early date – we get a typical mediaeval moated manor-house.'

According to Leland, the building was still sound during the reign of Henry VIII (1509–1547), but it was derelict a century later and without the smallest vestige remaining in 1791 (Crosfield, 1791). The moated enclosure, or bailey, was being used as a cemetery when I'Anson visited the site: 'A stranger to the North Riding as he is whirled northwards in an express from York to Darlington, may be excused if he were to form the opinion that the district is singularly devoid of mediaeval military remains. The only relic of the kind he will come to notice is a slighted motte and a moated cemetery at Northallerton which marks the site of the bishops of Durham.'

PICKERING
The ancient and pleasant market town of Pickering lies at the intersection of two ancient routes: one (north to south) linking the castles of Foss, Cropton and Malton, and the other (east to west) linking Helmsley, Brompton and Scarborough fortresses. Nestled on the southern edge of the North York Moors some 27 miles northeast of York, the town is a popular destination for visitors to the moors, especially those who love steam railways. The single branch line of the North Yorkshire Moors Railway, on which steam railway enthusiasts can still travel back as well as forward in time, follows the course of Pickering Beck to Grosmont. With the impressive ruins of Pickering Castle as a backdrop, few visitors will fail to notice this splendid stone edifice, which was developed in masonry in the late twelfth century. However, many will perhaps fail to notice or realise the significance of a distant hill on the opposite bank of the beck.

I'Anson was undecided as to whether the motte on the top of Beacon Hill represented the original stronghold erected by the Conqueror, or merely represented the site of a siege castle. In fact, little is known about the history of this earthwork situated in a quiet

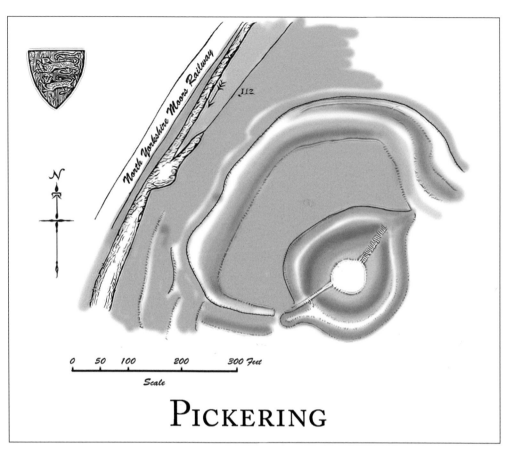

North Yorkshire Moors Railway

112

N

0   50   100   200   300 Feet

Scale

PICKERING

backwater to the west of the town centre. Beacon Hill overlooks what is effectively the extreme southern end of Newton Dale, a gorge through which melt water flooded down to form a huge lake at the end of the last Ice Age. Pickering Castle, on the opposite bank, is hardly a 'secret castle', but nevertheless one that was originally built of earth and timber and for this reason has been included here. Attributed to the Conqueror and commanding equally extensive views as Beacon Hill opposite, the fortress at Pickering originally comprised a motte and inner bailey. I'Anson considered it a fine example of the gradual evolution of an early Norman earth and timber stronghold into a shell-keep fortress. In 1154 a strong palisade would have stood where the present curtain wall stands. The motte, which would also have been crowned by a strong palisade, had a timber keep before masonry was introduced between 1182 and 1186. 'Henry II appears to have

Beacon Hill (in the far distance, centre) as viewed from the entrance to Pickering Castle.

converted the stronghold into a stone castle by erecting a wall round the original bailey, and it seems very probable that he, at the same time, added the outer or southern bailey, which he would defend with timber palisading,' suggested I'Anson. 'The masonry of the outer bailey was not erected until the reign of Edward II, during which time the shell keep would also have been erected.' Edward II was murdered in 1327 at the age of 43 and did indeed undertake major building work in the years immediately before his death.

The castle was in royal hands until 1267 when it passed (along with the title earl of Lancaster) to Edmund Crouchback, the younger son of Henry III. Edmund's son Thomas succeeded him, but in 1296 his estates reverted to the king until 1326 when his younger brother Henry was awarded his brother's titles and estates. In 1351 the castle became part of the Duchy of Lancaster, which in 1413 reverted to the Crown.

PICKHILL

Pickhill is a small village that lies close to the River Swale to the west of Thirsk. 'The site of this castle is pleasantly situated amid gently undulating country on the banks of the Pickhill Beck,' wrote I'Anson more than a century ago. But the peace of this rural backwater, just a mile from the busy A1, was promptly interrupted when the Steam Age arrived during the mid-nineteenth century. 'The earthworks, like those at Kildale and Northallerton (Castle Hills), have suffered much at the hands of the railway engineer,' continued I'Anson, 'and the motte, which is, like that of Whorlton, squarish in shape, is cut completely in two by the North Eastern Railway, and now forms part of the railway embankment.' Was this mutilation simply the mark of progress, or did the railway engineers receive special encouragement from the locals? I'Anson claimed that tales relating to hidden riches abound where mottes are concerned: 'There was a local tradition that Mother Shipton prophesied that the village of Pickhill would never prosper until "Pict's

The motte at Pickhill with the disused railway embankment running left to right through its centre.

The adjacent churchyard offers a better vantage point for viewing Pickhill motte.

Hill" or "Money Hill" as the motte is called to this day by the villagers, was cut open, and a legend existed that there was a chamber in the centre of the motte in which was a large oak chest, with three locks containing untold treasure. Numerous similar traditions exist, especially in Wales, with regard to the mottes of Early Norman castles. In 1851 the Leeds and Thirsk Railway Company cut open the motte before finally making it part of their embankment. Needless to say, although the motte was cut through in all directions and right down to its base, no treasure was found; the excavation, however, served to establish the fact that no masonry had existed. In the motte ditch were found fragments of cooking utensils, portions of tiling, a small brick, and a thin piece of iron, which had evidently once formed part of a mediaeval helmet. A local tradition still exists to the effect that "once upon a time" a great battle took place at this place, and may refer to the capture and destruction of the castle by the Scots.'

I'Anson believed that the fortress at Pickhill was founded by Roald, son of Hascoit (or Harsculf) Musard and third hereditary constable of Richmond Castle. When Roald's granddaughter married into the Neville family, the manor and fortress passed to her husband, Jollan de Neville, where it was occupied until 1319 when the village was sacked and destroyed by the Scots. The Church of All Saints, which is immediately next to the earthworks and contemporary with them, is worth a visit and contains the mutilated effigy of a knight bearing the arms of the Nevilles of Pickhill and thought by I'Anson to date between 1290 and 1310. Rural serenity has long since been restored to Pickhill. The railway line dissecting the castle site was closed in 1969 and subsequently dismantled as a consequence of the Beeching report.

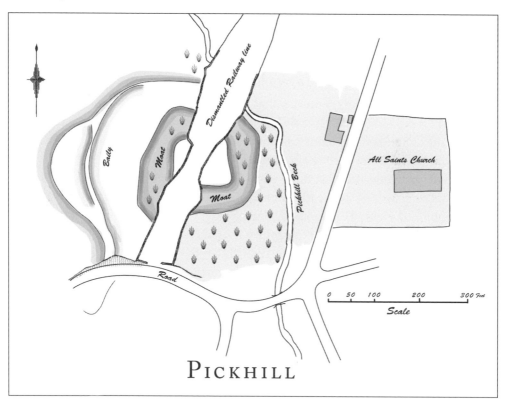

PICKHILL

The site is in a field close to the church and easily viewed from the churchyard. The old railway line, now heavily overgrown, dissects the motte roughly in the direction of the road running past the church to Highfield Farm. The railway embankment ends abruptly at the rear of a modern house, which conceals the motte from the village main street. Half expecting the house to be appropriately named 'Money Hill', the author was informed that this would not have gone down well with the neighbours.

PONTEFRACT

The historic market town of Pontefract lies in West Yorkshire close to the crossing point of the A1 or Great North Road and the M62 motorway. It is famous for its castle, which although attracting more than 65,000 visitors annually, is mentioned briefly here because it was originally an earth and timber fortress. Attributed to Ilbert de Lacy, the motte and bailey castle overlooks All Saints Church in the town centre and was built before 1086 on an ancient Saxon site known at the time of the Domesday Book as Tateshale (Tanshelf). Except for a brief period during the reign of Henry I (1100–1135), the de Lacys occupied the castle for more than two centuries and it was during the twelfth and early thirteenth centuries that the castle was rebuilt in stone. In 1311 it passed by marriage to Thomas of Lancaster, who was executed in 1322 and had his lands seized by the king. But five years later his titles and estates were restored to the family and in 1315 his nephew Henry became the first duke of Lancaster. After Henry's death the Lancaster estates passed by marriage to John of Gaunt and in 1399 John's son Henry Bolingbroke became king, making Pontefract a royal castle. During the sixteenth century it gradually fell into decay and it wasn't until shortly before the English Civil War that refurbishment work was carried out on what would become a Royalist garrison. The castle withstood siege after siege, but finally surrendered in 1649 and was dismantled by Parliament. It remains the property of the Duchy of Lancaster. Once one of the most important fortresses in the country, the castle site offers superb views of the town and surrounding area. Admission is free.

RAVENSWORTH

The pretty village of Ravensworth lies in semi-moorland about 4 miles northwest of Richmond in an area known as the Holme Valley or Holmedale. Situated close to a Roman road (Watling Street) and Holme Beck, a minor tributary of the River Swale, the village is home to the former stronghold of the FitzHugh family. The substantial masonry remains are on the southern fringe of the village but underlying them is a motte and bailey castle that was built here during the reign of Henry II (1154–1189). At the time of the Domesday Book, the honour of Richmond was held by Count Alan, as were the other manors in this parish. When Hugh, a descendant of Count Alan's brother Bardulf, died in 1303–1304, his son and heir used the surname FitzHugh. The FitzHughs were a notable family. Many featured prominently in the history of England and were buried at Jervaux Abbey. Among them was Henry, Lord FitzHugh, who was at Agincourt with Henry V and took 66 men-at-arms and 209 archers. The lands

Ravensworth Castle was once surrounded by a marsh or shallow lake.

remained in the FitzHugh family until 1513 when the last male heir, George, 8th Lord FitzHugh died without issue. His lands were divided and passed to his aunt and a cousin, Sir Thomas Parr, Lord of Kendal in Westmorland, who received the manor of Ravensworth. Thomas died in 1517 and his son William inherited. But in 1553 William was attainted for his support of Lady Jane Grey and although he was eventually pardoned in 1558 by Elizabeth I, he died without issue and his lands subsequently passed to the Crown. There they remained until 1625 when they were sold by Charles I to the City of London (Page, 1914).

At the time of his itineraries (1539–1543), Leland visited the castle and found it unexceptional. 'Ravenswarthe Castel, in a mares grownde [marish ground], and a parke on a litle hanging grownde by it . . . Lord Parr is owner therof. The castel, excepting 2 or 3 square towers, and a faire stable, with a conduct [conduit] cumming to the haull-side, hath nothing memorable.' About 1598 antiquarian William Camden also paid a visit: 'Ravensworth Castle rears its head with a large extent of ruinous walls, which had barons of its own, named Fitz Hugh, of old Saxon descent . . . and famous to the time of Henry VII, for their great estates acquired by marriage with the heiresses of the illustrious families of Furneaux and Marmion, which at the last came by females to the Fienes, Lords Dacre of the South, and to the Parrs.' (Mackenzie, 1896).

The motte of the original earth and timber fortress can still be identified underneath the masonry of the gateway tower at the northern end of the earthwork. In earlier times the site would have been partially surrounded by a marsh or shallow lake. There is no record of when works in masonry commenced, but in 1391, Henry, Lord FitzHugh received a licence to enclose 200 acres of parkland, by which time it is more than likely that stone would have been used to strengthen the castle. This theory is supported by the architecture of some of the surviving stonework, which suggests that the castle itself was rebuilt during this time. The estate went into decline after it was divided in 1512 and became nothing more than a stone quarry for the local populace. Significant parts of the standing remains, including the gate tower, are at risk according to a survey report dated 2008. Interestingly the 2m-high medieval hunting park wall built in 1391 can still be traced for most of its length. It has been partly rebuilt on the original line, but many stretches have survived in the original medieval form.

The ruins, which are on private land, are clearly visible in a field to the immediate southeast of the village and can be viewed from a public right of way.

ROUGEMONT

The remains of the earth and timber ringwork fortress known as Rougemont Castle are on the steep northern bank of the River Wharfe just to the north of Leeds and southeast of Weeton village. The site, which might have been occupied as early as in prehistoric times, overlooks a sharp bend in the river and is located in a densely wooded area, a mere stone's throw away from Harewood House. In 1859, the antiquary John Jones wrote in praise of the scenery but lamented the coming of the railways: 'The village of Harewood is pleasantly situated on the Leeds and Harrogate road, about eight miles distant from each town. Its position is one of great beauty, standing on a considerable eminence overlooking the valley of the Wharfe. To the west a prospect of a most diversified character presents itself embracing the magnificent scenery of Wharfedale, for nearly 20 miles, bounded in the distance by the hills of Craven; while to the east the vale of York lays stretched out before the observer, York Minster being clearly discernible at the distance of 20 miles. Standing at the intersection of two highroads, the great North Road, and the highway from the west to York, it was formerly a place of much life and bustle, twenty-two stagecoaches passing and repassing every day. The railroads however has destroyed this traffic and one solitary stager to Harrogate during the summer season, is all that remains.'

At some date before 1087, Duke William gave Harewood, with the honour of Skipton and other large estates in Yorkshire, to Robert de Romelli. When Robert's two sons died without issue, it passed by the marriage of his eldest daughter to William, Earl of Chester and then to William de Curci, the son of Robert's second eldest daughter. It passed by marriage again to Waryn FitzGerald, chamberlain to King John, and to Baldwyn de Redvers (also spelt Rivers or Ripariis) who died in 1216. His wife, Margery FitzGerald, married Fulk de Breant, a favourite of King John whose name became de Insula or de Lisle due to his large estates in the Isle of Wight. And it is to his line that the ancient fortress at Rougemont is attributed. The honour passed briefly to William de Fortibus, Earl of Albermarle, Lord of Holderness and Skipton upon his marriage to Baldwyn's sister, Isabella. But when he died in 1260 his only surviving child, a daughter called Aveline, was too young to inherit and became a ward of the Crown. She grew to be both beautiful and immensely wealthy. Upon reaching the age of 18 she was married to Edmund Crouchback, Earl of Lancaster, in the presence of the king, queen and almost all the nobility of the kingdom (Jones, 1859).

Rougemont Castle is now overgrown with trees. The ringwork and broad surrounding ditch lie within a bailey that would probably have been entered from the west through a gap in the bank and ditch. Traces of buildings can still be identified within the bailey and hints of a wall section suggest that the castle was reinforced with masonry at some stage, probably in 1365 when Sir William de Aldburgh bought the manor from his brother-in-law. Outside the bailey is another outwork protected to the west and south by a tributary of the River Wharfe and to the east by the bailey embankment. North of this is a marshy area believed to represent fishponds. The site was probably abandoned about 1366 when nearby Harewood Castle was built by the de Lisle family. In 1738 the Lascelles family acquired the estate and in 1759 commenced building Harewood House.

In 1859, John Jones visited the castle and wrote, 'The area which the building occupied is about eighty yards by sixty, the whole of which is moated round. Nothing is left by which an approximation could be made of its size, plan or appearance; the very stones are gone, the mounds alone remaining to indicate its site. An immense rampart encompasses the whole, forming three sides of an oblong or rectangle, nearly a mile in length, and in some places 18 feet broad. The whole of the earthworks are in an excellent state of preservation, and well worth a visit from the antiquary.'

SANDAL

Sandal, or Sandal Magma to be precise, is an ancient town situated 2 miles south of Wakefield on the Wakefield to Barnsley road and close to the River Calder. When William de Warenne, 2nd Earl of Surrey was granted lands here in 1107, he chose Sandal as his caput for the manor of Wakefield and built a motte and bailey castle on a sandstone ridge with a commanding view over his considerable estate. As the castle is barely a mile from a motte and bailey fortress known as Lowe Hill on the opposite bank of the Calder, there is a theory that they were intentionally built to jointly command the river valley. Despite lying close to the centre of the town, the highly visible and imposing ruins at Sandal are pleasantly surrounded by open fields to the north, west and south. The earthworks, which are in excellent condition and in the main complete, comprise the original motte, inner bailey, associated ditchwork and counterscarp bank. A wooden tower would have stood on the motte originally, but this was replaced in the thirteenth century by the masonry shell keep that remains today.

William died in 1138 and was succeeded by his eldest son, William, 3rd Earl of Surrey, who died on the Second Crusade in 1148. His title and lands then passed by the marriage of his daughter to Hamelin Plantagenet, a half-brother of Henry II to whom the first masonry additions to Sandal Castle are attributed. He adopted the family name of de Warenne and the castle remained in the family until after the death of John de Warennes, 7th Earl of Surrey. John was godfather to Edmund of Langley, Duke of York, who in 1353 was granted all the earl's lands north of the Trent. Sandal figured prominently among the residences of Richard, Duke of York, but when he and his son Edmund, Earl of Rutland were killed in 1460 at the Battle of Wakefield, the duke's eldest son, Edward, inherited. A mere two weeks later, Edward triumphed at the Battle of Towton and became Edward IV – the first Yorkist monarch. The Council of the North, set up by Edward IV at the beginning of 1472 under the presidency of Richard, Duke of Gloucester (later Richard III), also met here. Sandal remained in the hands of the Crown until 1566 when it passed to the Duchy of Lancaster, but by 1592 it had been rendered a ruin by successive (negligent) private owners. Garrisoned by Royalists during the English

Civil War, it was twice besieged and further damaged by cannon fire before being left to the ravages of nature. Once completely overgrown except for a few wall fragments to the south, it was partially excavated in the late nineteenth century. The castle is now integrated into a public park, which like the castle is open to visitors.

SAXTON

The historic village of Saxton lies in lovely countryside about 4 miles from Tadcaster and 15 miles southwest of York. A motte and bailey fortress once stood here and although little is known about its origin, the remains can still be seen in a field to the southeast of All Saints Church. A medieval manor house (demolished in the nineteenth century) to the immediate south of Manor Farm has disturbed the original earthworks, but the low, wide motte with surrounding ditch are clearly identifiable in the northwestern sector of a rectangular bailey. Although the ramparts have been largely altered by their incorporation into later land boundaries, the extent of the bailey can be traced. To the east it manifests as a slight bank running from Fircroft to Manor Farm, to the west by the line of Main Street, and to the north and south by the boundaries of adjacent properties. A bank and ditch just inside the eastern bailey boundary is thought to be associated with the later medieval manor house. Formerly owned by the Hungate family, the foundations of the manor house still survive today. A disused track leading to it runs diagonally across the bailey at a tangent to the motte. To the west of this are other smaller features considered the remains of gardens or house plots associated either with the manor house or with the medieval village.

Britain's bloodiest battle took place on unenclosed land to the north of the village on 29 March (Palm Sunday) 1461 during which rival Lancastrian and Yorkist forces fought all day in what famously became known as the Battle of Towton. Towton Heath, where the battle was actually fought, lies between the villages of Saxton and Towton and there is a commemorative walk around part of the battlefield. Re-enactments of the battle also take place during the year. More than 35,000 Englishmen died on that unhappy day and the old English aristocracy was all but annihilated. Chroniclers affirmed that the Cock

Beck was choked with the bodies of the dead and dying, and was 'collored with bloud' for more than a mile below its confluence with the Wharfe. Great trenches were dug to receive the bodies of the slain, one of which is on the north side of Saxton churchyard, where Ralph, Lord Dacre lies buried. His tomb remained in a neglected state until 1883, when Lord Carlisle of Castle Howard had it restored. Many relics have been found on and around the battle site, including weaponry, coins, spurs and a massive, gold signet ring (Speight, 1902).

For those in need of refreshments, the picturesque Greyhound pub won't disappoint.

SCARBOROUGH

Standing on a rocky promontory overlooking the North Sea, the ruined rectangular keep at Scarborough Castle is the perfect backdrop to this popular Yorkshire resort. Excavations here have turned up evidence of settlements dating back to the late Bronze Age and to Roman occupation up to the fifth century. The stone keep dates back to between 1158 and 1174, but on or about 1135 one of the most powerful of the Yorkshire barons is thought to have built a timber fortress here, which is why this prominent edifice receives a brief mention. The original earth and timber construction theory is supported by a text in the *Chronicle of Meaux* [Melsa] *Abbey*, which describes the tower at the entrance as being decayed and fallen when the king seized it. 'William, surnamed Le Gros, Earl of Albermarle and Holderness, observing this place to be admirably situated for the erection of a castle, increased the great natural strength of it by a very costly work, having enclosed the all the plain upon the rock by a wall, and built a tower at the entrance. But this being decayed and fallen, King Henry II commanded a great and strong castle to be built upon the same spot.' As this was just 20 years after its construction, I'Anson reasoned that this was far too short a period of time for anything but a timber keep to have decayed. He proposed that it probably stood on or near the site of the present stone tower and might have contained the earl's private apartments. Protected only by perimeter defences – mainly a ditch and palisaded embankment that cut off the headland from the mainland – the castle surrendered to Henry II in 1155 at a time when it comprised

Dawn at Scarborough Castle: an ancient text suggests that it was originally an earth and timber fortress.

little more than a 'strongly walled enclosure, devoid of a stone keep' (I'Anson). Major rebuilding work took place when Scarborough became a royal castle and the keep and curtain wall visible today date back to this period. King John visited the castle four times between 1201 and 1216, as did Edward II a century later. During the English Civil War, the castle was a Royalist stronghold and Parliamentary forces laid siege to it in July 1645 using the roof of the adjacent parish church of St Mary's as an artillery platform. The castle exchanged hands a couple of times up to 1648 and the keep sustained the major damage still visible today during this period. Further information about the history of Scarborough Castle can be found in the ample literature available to visitors.

SEDBERGH

Sedbergh is a small market town that lies 12 miles east of Kendal in the Yorkshire Dales National Park. Nestled among the fells at a point where four rivers and dales meet, Sedbergh was once the place where ancient and important trade routes from Kendal to York and Lancaster to Newcastle converged. Splendid views can be had from the fells above Sedbergh and from the lie of the land one can easily imagine why the Normans chose to build a motte and bailey fortress at this strategically important location. Known as Castlehaw or Castlehaugh Tower, the earthworks stand sentinel above the centre and to the eastern side of Sedbergh and command the river crossing below. In 1872 the Reverend William Thompson wrote, 'The chief coefficients of our ever-varying, ever-beautiful scenery are the mountains, which stand round about like protecting giants, and the becks, which leap and tumble down their sides to the valley steams, as they hurry onwards to join the brimming Lune. The scenic attractions of the district must be visited to be appreciated, for no amount of ornamental epithets can convey to a third person a true idea of their varied loveliness.'

The Reverend Thompson's recommendation is as valid today as it was more than a century ago. Indeed, the motte of Castlehaw itself offers commanding views over both the town and down to the Lune Valley, and beyond. Rather surprisingly, little is known about the castle site or indeed the ancient settlement of the area other than that there are some mounds associated with the Iron Age in nearby Dentdale to the immediate south. The Castlehaw site is thought to have Saxon origins and the Romans also left their mark near here when they built a branch road from the Lune valley that passes through Sedbergh. Thompson wrote, 'The situation of Castlehaw is such a prominent feature in the landscape at Sedbergh, near the track of this cross-road, would suggest the possibility of it having been a Roman exploratory mound originally, though this view in no way militates against its subsequent adoption as the site of a Saxon stronghold.' The Vikings also made their presence felt when they migrated inland from the west coast to plunder and find new grazing pastures. In fact, it has been suggested that the name Sedbergh actually derives from the Old Norse language.

Whatever its origin, the oval motte at Castlehaw is partially surrounded by a wide ditch except to the south where the ground falls steeply away. To the north and east there is a partial bank outside the ditch and there are traces of a small bailey to the west of the motte. In 1938 a Royal Observer Corps monitoring post was built on the motte, which saw service during the Second World War. During the Cold War, a subterranean monitoring post existed here until 1968. This was subsequently removed, which accounts for a hollow that remains in the earthwork today. When the castle was destroyed or abandoned is unknown and no masonry has been found on the site either before or during repairs in 1994.

It is thought that the castle was the work of Robert de Mowbray in about 1092, which roughly coincides with the period that Castle Howe was erected in Kendal. At the time of the Domesday Book, the vill of Sedbergh contained four carucates of land and was part of the 'Terra Regis' (king's land) given to Robert de Mowbray, Earl of Northumberland. It then passed by marriage to Nigel de Albini, who subsequently changed his name to de Mowbray. Nigel's son, Roger, inherited and held the whole of the Wapentake of Ewecross in the reign of Henry I (1100–1135). During the reign of King John (1199–1216), the manors of Sedbergh, Garsdale and Dent passed to Adam de Staveley, upon whose death in 1225 without a male heir they passed to Henry FitzRanulph, Lord of Ravensworth through the marriage of his daughter, Alicia. The manors remained with Henry's descendants in the name of FitzHugh until the reign of Henry VI (1422–1461). The lordship then became shared until 1596, when Sir Thomas Strickland of Sizergh Castle bought it from joint owners, thus reuniting the manorial fragments (Thompson, 1892). It remained in his family's possession until the Reverend Thompson's day.

SELBY

The small but historic town of Selby is home to one of Yorkshire's hidden gems and deserves a somewhat longer introduction. Located on the west bank of the River Ouse, 12 miles south of York, Selby has an ancient abbey that has stood at the heart of this small community for almost 1,000 years. It was founded by St Benedict of Auxerre who came here from France following a vision he had of a place called Selebaie. Predating both York and Durham, it was the first monastery to be founded in the North of England after the Norman Conquest. Its fame increased when William the Conqueror's fourth son, Henry (later to become King Henry I of England), was born at the abbey in 1068. With royal assent, the abbey flourished and its twelfth- and fourteenth-century architectural features are still considered among the finest examples in England. Although Selby's name suggests a Viking origin, it is thought to be much older. One suggestion is that the town is actually 'Seletun', as referred to in the *Anglo-Saxon Chronicle*. But the Romans were also here and the name Salebeia fits with the Latin for willow (Salix), which would have abounded on the banks of the Ouse.

Selby also had a long-forgotten castle, of which there are, sadly, no visible remains. The only hint that a castle once stood here comes from the pen of an anonymous Selby monk. Writing in 1174, he described a time of baronial feuding during which Count William of Aumale captured the castle, which was built by Henry de Lacy. He was licensed to build a castle here soon after 1143 and the site is thought to have been located somewhere north of the abbey and close to the River Ouse, but the precise position remains a mystery. Henry de Lacy succeeded to the honour of Pontefract in 1142, so we must assume he built the castle as a matter of priority and perhaps to protect the abbey itself. Both the castle and abbey would have been constructed using timber and could have easily been burnt to the ground if left undefended.

Despite no castle earthworks to view, Selby's visitor-friendly abbey church is certainly well worth a visit and is open daily.

SHEFFIELD

Once located in a richly wooded area, Sheffield was at best a mere village when its castle stood on a steep-sided sandstone outcrop overlooking the confluence of the rivers Don and Sheaf. A deep and wide moat was dug to the south and west so that water from the two rivers surrounded the entire fortress (Hey, 2010). Even in medieval times the local mineral wealth had led to the manufacture of edged tools and weapons, such as arrowheads and spearheads. To this day a bundle of arrows is in Sheffield's coat of arms and crossed arrows form the badge of the ancient Cutlers' Company (Timbs and Gunn, 1872).

Attributed to William de Lovetot, lord of the manor of Hallamshire, and built during the reign of Henry I (1100–1135), the motte and bailey castle was first referred to in a return made by the sheriff of Derbyshire on or about 1188 (Hunter, 1819). In 1204 the castle passed by marriage to Gerard de Furnival, but was burnt down in 1266 – as was most of Sheffield itself – during the de Montfort rebellion against Henry III. In 1270, Thomas de Furnival received royal consent to rebuild the castle in stone and add battlements.

William, Lord Furnival died in 1383 without a male heir and his daughter married Sir Thomas Neville, who died in 1406. Thomas had an only daughter who married John Talbot, Earl of Shrewsbury. He was a soldier–statesman of some repute and his family succeeded to the manor and castle. At that time the castle was at the height of its powers and estimated to have covered an area of more than 4 acres. A large area of parkland extending from the castle for 4 miles in an easterly direction to the present village of Handsworth also belonged to the Talbot family. It was George Talbot, 4th Earl of Shrewsbury who built the nearby lodge called Sheffield Manor in 1516 and received Cardinal Wolsey there soon after Wolsey's apprehension. His namesake, the 6th earl, was appointed the custodian of Mary, Queen of Scots, who was held in both the castle and at the manor house by order of Queen Elizabeth I for 14 years between 1570 and 1584. In 1616 the Howard family, earls of Arundel and Surrey, held the castle until the English Civil War in 1642 when it was surrendered following a siege. Although being retaken by the Royalists a year later, Parliamentary forces laid siege again in 1644 and retook the castle before it was finally demolished between 1648 and 1649 by order of Parliament. Much of the stone was plundered and reused for construction in the city, as shown on the first detailed map of Sheffield dated 1736. A steelworks occupied the site until 1899, but in that year the city council bought the land from the duke of Norfolk and it was subsequently cleared and redeveloped by the city council.

Excavations carried out between 1927 and 1929 at what is still known as Castle Hill, revealed that the castle remains lie beneath a sizable area of the city centre now occupied by Castlegate, Exchange Street and Waingate up to the River Sheaf. They might even extend further westwards across Waingate (Armstrong, 1930). Masonry remains were uncovered, including one section of wall that had survived up to a height of 30ft. Also revealed were the wooden remains of a large, possibly Saxon structure, overlaid by a timber castle of a date commensurate with William de Lovetot's motte and bailey fortress. Roman and Saxon pottery, as well as a Bronze Age tool, were also found.

A section of masonry exposed during excavations was still visible in a cellar of the Castle Market until it closed in November 2013. In 2014 plans were announced to rebuild the castle entrance in connection with a multimillion-pound regeneration scheme in the city's Castlegate area.

SHERIFF HUTTON

The historic village of Sheriff Hutton lies about 10 miles north of York and is the site of two castles: an early Norman motte and bailey stronghold built c.1100 and a fourteenth-century quadrangular palace -fortress. The former's intriguing earthwork, to which there is public access, lies just to the south of the parish church and is attributed to the former sheriff of Yorkshire, Aschetil de Bulmer. However, I'Anson thought that Aschetil's son Bertram actually built the castle in 1140, as first proposed by antiquarian William Camden (1551–1623). Whatever the truth, the manor passed by marriage to Geoffrey de Neville upon Bertram's death and it remained occupied by the family until 1382, when work began on the nearby palace-fortress.

The earthwork struck I'Anson as marking a new and unusual type of earth and timber castle, where buildings are deeply sunk within the motte itself. 'A motte of some size enclosing a very small ward surrounded by an abnormally high banquette, which appears absolutely colossal when compared with the miniature court beneath. In three places this banquette presents huge gaps, which gave an extraordinary bastion-like appearance to the motte. The gap on the west represents the entrance to the summit of the motte from the attached bailey. The timber walls of the keep would rest upon the banquette, the well-like ward or court forming the basement of the

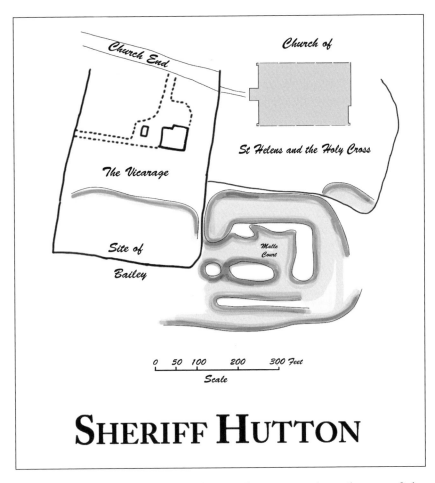

Church End

Church of

St Helens and the Holy Cross

The Vicarage

Site of

Bailey

Motte Court

0   50 100   200   300 Feet
Scale

SHERIFF HUTTON

tower.' I'Anson traced the bailey to the west and northwest of the motte, but even 100 years ago its ditches had been largely filled in.

Equally intriguing are the nearby remains of the once-impressive late fourteenth-century quadrangular palace-fortress built by John, Lord Neville of Raby. The Council of the North, set up in 1472 by Edward IV to improve government control and economic prosperity for the benefit of Northern England, was first held here under the presidency of Edward's brother Richard, Duke of Gloucester (later Richard III). Overlooking the Vale of York, the ruins are now reduced to mere remnants of the former palace. Once held by Richard Neville, Earl of Warwick of 'Warwick the Kingmaker' fame, it was seized by the Crown upon his death and given to Richard, Duke of Gloucester before being eventually abandoned and sold as a ruin in 1618–1619.

Good views can be had from the public footpath around the ruin, which is itself on private land.

Take the opportunity to visit the adjacent 900-year-old church of St Helen and the Holy Cross in which an interesting tomb effigy can be found. I'Anson dated the effigy to between 1350 and 1360 and suggested it represents Edmund de Thweng of Cornborough.

SKELTON

Situated not far from the Yorkshire coast and just to the southwest of Saltburn-by-the-Sea is the village of Skelton where an earth and timber fortress once existed. Built by Richard de Surdeval about 1072–1075, it was granted to the de Brus family at some time between 1100 and 1119. They developed it in stone between 1190 and 1200, but what remains today bears no resemblance to the earlier de Brus castle by all accounts. In a letter to John Walker Ord, author of *The History and Antiquities of Cleveland* (1846), a West Riding clergyman once wrote despairingly, 'The old castle, built around 1140, was a beautiful specimen of antiquity and picturesque loveliness, being surrounded by a deep glen, finely wooded. In 1788 the grandson of John Hall, who assumed the name of Wharton, commenced the work of destruction and at an enormous expense contrived to flood the glen, demolish the terraces, pull down every remnant of Norman antiquity, including a magnificent tower, and has left behind him the most extraordinary specimen of folly and bad taste to be found in the whole country.'

Situated at the nab end of a long promontory and occupying some 5^1/$_2$ acres, the original castle was by far the largest in area of the timber castles of the North Riding. I'Anson was in no doubt about the suitability of its location: 'The modern castellated building is beautifully situated on the site of the ancient fortress. Below the castle is a deep, heavily-wooded glen, which winds down to the sea with the pretty little watering place of Saltburn-by-the-Sea on its banks.' According to I'Anson, a broad ditch was originally cut across the promontory, but this has since been filled in. The approach to the castle, however, has remained unchanged through the centuries. 'The entrance to this large, fortified enclosure was from the south by a paved bridle path, still bearing the name of Borough-gate. The stockaded enclosure was evidently almost exactly at the point where the road known as "Church Lane" now meets the highroad from Skelton to Guisborough, and here was a small triangular-shaped outwork or barbican, which would certainly be defended by palisading. From this fortified outwork, a gate, almost on the site of the gate now leading into the grounds of the present caste, gave access to the large communal fortified enclosure, or burgus.' As at Whorlton, the defensive enclosure contained the church and village. 'Around and about the church would cluster the timber huts of the burgus or village. The enclosure would be defended by timber palisading crowning the summit of the scarped sides of the ravine or dry ditch on either side.'

In 1272 the ancient stone castle passed by marriage to Walter de Fauconberg, whose family held it for five generations. It passed again by marriage to Sir William Neville and later John, Lord Conyers, who died in 1556 without a male heir. The estate was divided among his three daughters and remained in their families until being sold to Robert Trotter in 1577. His family resided there until 1727 when it passed by marriage to Joseph Hall, whose grandson, John Hall Stevenson (later named Wharton), drastically changed the castle. 'The work of destruction, which was carried out only too thoroughly, took place between 1788 and 1794, when not only was the entire feudal castle pulled down, but all irregularities in the ground were carefully levelled,' recounted I'Anson. It was only with the aid of an eighteenth-century drawing that I'Anson was able to suggest that the original earthworks had featured a motte at all. 'Hall-Stevenson's drawing would rather suggest that the rectangular keep might have been erected on a lowered motte. If one existed, it would be of small size and would certainly have been placed at the northern or nab end of the promontory.' The castellated building now occupying the site is in private hands and the grounds are, regrettably, not open to the public.

SKIPSEA

'One of the most interesting of the late 11th-century castles of the East Riding,' is how I'Anson described the earthworks at Skipsea 100 years ago. Situated barely a stone's throw away from the sea on glacial deposits left by the Ice Age, this former seat of the lords of Holderness

The motte at Skipsea is visible from a number of directions, but the site is best approached and viewed from the west where access is the easiest.

was literally an island linked to the sea by a waterway before drainage was undertaken early in the eighteenth century. Indeed, the majority of the low-lying land east of the River Hull is thought to have been little more than a swamp when the Normans invaded. Despite the passage of time, it does not take much imagination to picture the motte at Skipsea surrounded by a mere and connected to the bailey by a narrow timber bridge.

'Close to Skipsea is Skipsea Brough, which contains a remarkable series of British earthworks, and a central mound, which were occupied by Drogo in the time of William the Norman, and upon which are yet the remains of his keep,' wrote Driffield-born antiquary Thomas Sheppard in 1912. The high rate of coastal erosion in Holderness suggests that the sea has made an inroad of at least 3¹/₂ miles since Roman times. So much so that three villages to the east of Skipsea have been lost to the sea over the centuries. Indeed, the encroachment of the sea was measured to be higher than average along

Stream Dike, which flows left to right at the bottom of the field, runs close to Skipsea motte on the eastern side.

this section of the Holderness coast. 'During 111 years the average rate of erosion of the land at Skipsea was (according to Pickwell in 1878) just under 2 yards a year,' continued Sheppard. 'Mr. Hatfield measured the distance from the windmill at Skipsea to the sea in 1833, and it was 1757 yards. This windmill has now gone, but I am informed by the Reverend R.W. Watson that its site was, in February 1912, 225 yards nearer the sea than in 1833, which is a loss of three yards a year for 79 years.' Skipsea Marr, the mere that once existed here, was well stocked with fish in 1288 and would certainly have been some distance inland from the cliff edge in the thirteenth century (Sheppard, 1912).

Built about 1086 by Flemish nobleman Dru de la Beuvriere (also spelt Drogo Beavriere), the motte and bailey fortress erected on the site of much older earthworks was the original headquarters of the seigneury of Holderness, although it is not certain whether the bailey was part of the original eleventh-century castle. A tiny section of a former wing wall made from mortar and cobbles can still be found on the east side of the motte, but the lack of foundations on the summit suggests that the keep was never developed in masonry. Cobbled stones are evident in many of the village houses, but how many actually came from the beach and not the castle is unlikely to be answered. I'Anson thought that any works in masonry were unlikely to have occurred before 1155, the year in which William le Gros lost Scarborough Castle.

Shortly after it was built, the castle's founder allegedly poisoned his wife, who unfortunately for him was the niece of William the Conqueror. Fortunately for him, he absconded before the news reached the Conqueror, but his lands were confiscated in his absence and handed to Odo, Count of Champagne and Aumale, husband of the Conqueror's sister, Adelaide. Less than a decade later, Odo and his son were themselves imprisoned for conspiracy. Their lands were subsequently handed to Arnold de Montgomery, who held the castle until Henry I granted it to Odo's son, Stephen, Count of Aumale, in whose family it remained until 1221. Stephen's eldest son and heir, William le Gros (founder of Scarborough Castle), succeeded him and in turn the castle passed by marriage to William de Forz I and then to his son. Following a rebellion against the Crown in 1221, Henry III

An impression of the first earth and timber fortress at Skipsea.

ordered the castle to be demolished, but when William's son died abroad in 1241, the title and lands reverted to William's grandson. Less than a decade later the castle was abandoned when the family moved its household to Burstwick, near Kingston Upon Hull. In 1840, Poulson wrote, 'It is greatly to be regretted that so little information exists relative to the occasional residences of the Earls of Albemarle, as it is evident that they had a mansion here at a very early period, soon after the demolition of the Castle of Skipsea.'

SKIPTON

Referred to as the gateway to the Dales, Skipton is a sizeable market town on the River Aire and the Leeds and Liverpool Canal to the south of the Yorkshire Dales. The formidable Skipton Castle, which is one of the most complete and best-preserved medieval castles in England, receives a brief mention here because it was originally an earth and timber fortress. Sadly no traces of the original fortress remain, but it was erected about 1090 possibly due to its commanding position close to two important Roman road junctions and a pass through the Pennines. Attributed to Robert de Romille, it would have originally comprised merely a wooden stockade and as there is no trace of a motte it is highly probable that this was found unneccesary due to it being perched high above Eller Beck with the steep natural defences. In 1102, Robert's lands were extended to include all of Upper Wharfedale and Airedale, but after his death the title and honour of Skipton passed by marriage of his daughter and heiress, Cecilia, to the earl of Albermarle's line. It passed to the Crown during the period of a ward's minority, but by 1310, Skipton Castle was in the hands of Robert de Clifford, 1st Lord Clifford of Skipton. He ordered works to strengthen the castle, but was killed at the Battle of Bannockburn before work was completed. The castle remained in the Royalist Clifford family's possession and although slighted by Cromwell during the Civil War (it was the last Royalist bastion in the north to yield and only did so in 1645 after a three-year siege), it was restored and remained the Cliffords' main seat until 1676. The existing stone edifice is one of the best-preserved medieval castles, not just in Yorkshire but in the entire land, and is open to visitors the whole year round.

SOWERBY

The village of Sowerby (Sorebi in the Domesday Book) lies just to the west of Sowerby Bridge and almost 4 miles southwest of Halifax. Once known as the Forest of Sowerbyshire, the land around Sowerby on the south bank of the River Calder and the west bank of the River Ryburn was once a royal chase. Offering outstanding views over the Calder valley, one can easily imagine why Sowerby was chosen as the site of a motte castle in what was once a manor that belonged to the lordship of Wakefield. Known locally as Castle Hill, the earthworks are attributed to the earls of Warenne and Surrey, and are in a field to the north of Town Gate. The forest of Sowerbyshire was bestowed upon William, 1st Earl of Warenne for his support of the Conqueror during the Norman invasion. Traces of the deer park can still be found to this day along the River Calder in the shape of boundary markers (standing stones) marked with the letter 's' denoting Sowerby. William, 2nd Earl of Warenne is known to have built a motte and bailey castle (Lowe Hill) at Thornes near Wakefield before his death in 1138 and so might have been responsible for building the timber fortress at Sowerby. The family later built the timber castle at Sandal, which became the caput for its Wakefield manor estates from about 1240. The motte at Sowerby, which is much silted down and now barely the size of a low hillock, still commands a prominent position over the surrounding land and the wide ditch is still traceable. The entrance is presumed to have been on the southwest side where there are hints of a former causeway.

SWINE

The site known as Castle Hill, which lies to the southwest of the ancient village of Swine and close to where the disused Hull–Hornsea railway line and Holderness Drain intersect, is thought to be all that remains of a former motte and bailey castle. Its precise origin is unknown, but Richard and Hugh de Verli were the first known tenants of Swine following the Norman Conquest, and Robert de Verli (probably a relative and possibly the son of Hugh de Verli) was the founder of the Cistercian priory at Swine in or about 1150. The manor subsequently passed by marriage to the Hilton family in whose possession it remained until the middle of the fifteenth century. A clue to the castle's origin, however, might lie in an ancient text from 1352 in which John de Sutton (1308–1356), lord of the manor of the nearby village of Sutton, was fined for building, crenellating and battlementing a castle at Braunceholm (Patent Rolls, Edward III). Sutton, Swine and modern-day Bransholme are more or less equidistant from Castle Hill and the suggestion has been made that Castle Hill might indeed be the 'Braunceholm' referred to in 1352. In 1918 excavations at Castle Hill revealed the corner of a building thought to be the remains of an old hall that might have been the residence of John de Sutton, whose family was among the earliest benefactors of Swine Priory. 'Branceholme or Braunceholm is frequently alluded to as belonging to the Suttons, lords of Sutton, although it would appear, originally, either in whole or part, to have been an appendage to Swine. The pasture of Branceholme is mentioned in 1218, as granted by Saer de Sutton to Walter Grey, Archbishop of York,' wrote Poulson (1840). The site is on private land but is visible from the disused railway line, which is a public right of way.

TADCASTER

The ancient market town of Tadcaster lies about 10 miles southwest of York and has been occupied since Roman times, when it was known as Calcaria and served as an important staging post at a crossing on the River Wharfe. The town is also mentioned in the *Anglo-Saxon Chronicle* as being the place used by King Harold to muster his forces and fleet before marching on York and joining battle at Stamford Bridge. But the English victory over the Norwegian force was short-lived and it was soon the Normans who occupied the town. Attributed to William de Percy and thought to have been built in the late eleventh century on pre-Norman defences, the remains of a motte and bailey castle are just to the north of St Mary's Church on the northeastern edge of the town. The motte is on the west bank of the Wharfe overlooking the river to the east, but was slighted on that side in the nineteenth century by the building of cottages, of which a brick wall is all that now remains. To the west there is a small inner bailey, which is separated from the outer bailey by a ditch that is infilled at the southern end. To the north of the outer bailey is a low bank and traces of an infilled moat can still be seen at the western end. These were excavated in the 1980s and showed that the ditch had curved around the bailey from north to south and been of considerable width and depth. The castle fell into decline when the Percy family deserted their Tadcaster residence in the twelfth century, but it was refortified in 1642 during the English Civil War. Small mounds to the west and northwest of the bailey possibly date back to this period. It is doubtful that the castle ever had works in masonry, but if it did, the stone might well have been reused, for instance in building a bridge.

THIRSK

The thriving market town of Thirsk lies between Northallerton and York in the Vale of Mowbray, which is distinguishable from the Vale of York by its meandering rivers and undulating landscape. The town is the site of a former motte and bailey castle attributed to Roger de Stuteville, which was erected about 1092. In 1857, Whellan wrote, 'This fine valley is scarcely to be equalled by any tract of country in the Kingdom,' and that the castle was, 'a very extensive fortress with numerous lofty towers and inferior to few in the Kingdom for the magnificence of its external appearance and the sumptuous grandeur of the interior'. A century ago I'Anson found a rather passive scene awaiting him: 'Thirsk is a pleasant but sleepy old town left stranded high and dry, as it were, by the railway; and from the few trains which, during the day, deign to stop at the distant station, an incongruous-looking motor bus conveys the long-suffering traveller to the town. Nor does the high road condescend to more than a nodding acquaintance with the slumbering town, for one merely catches a distant glimpse of the tower of the beautiful Perpendicular church as one motors from the north towards York. Possibly not one in a thousand who actually pass through the town has seen the scanty remains of the home of the Lady Gundreda and the famous Roger de Mowbray, of the once great castle of the historic house who gave their name to the pleasant vale of Mowbray.'

After the Battle of Tinchebrai, when de Stuteville was captured, a

A large Victorian villa now occupies the site known as Castle Garth, where traces of the earthwork can still be seen between the villa and the industrial building to the left.

portion of his estates including the fortress at Thirsk was handed to Nigel de Albini, who had greatly distinguished himself at Tinchebrai. Nigel was a cousin of Robert de Mowbray and when he died in 1136 the fortress passed to his widow's son, Roger, who assumed the Mowbray name. Of all the North Riding barons of his day, Mowbray appeared to be the most attractive, said I'Anson. 'He wins our interest from the first as the boy hero of the Battle of the Standard, he is not only famous for his unfailing generosity to monastic houses [he founded the abbeys at Byland and Newburgh], but as a distinguished warrior and Crusader.' But all did not end well because on his return from the Holy Land in 1174, he backed Prince Henry's attempt to seize his father's Crown and aided the Scottish invasion of the north of England. The Scottish king's capture in Alnwick proved a deathblow to the success of the revolt and Mowbray submitted to Henry II at Northampton. Although his surrender of Thirsk Castle gained him a pardon, the great timber castle, which had been Mowbray's favourite residence, was dismantled and destroyed in 1176.

By all accounts, Roger de Mowbray shared his mother's

compassion and generosity towards the clergy. I'Anson tells a nice tale (originally from Dugdale's *Monasticum Angelicum*, 1655–1673) of how in 1134 the monks of Furness, after being plundered and their house burnt by the Scots, were making their way to York and were intercepted by Gundreda's steward, who suggested they should call at Thirsk Castle. Watching them approach from an upper window of the fortress and pitying their miserable condition, Gundreda offered them shelter in the castle before placing them in the care of her relative Robert d'Alneto, the hermit of Hode or Hood Grange. Here they lived until a year or two later when Roger de Mowbray, the young heir, came of age. Roger generously gave them his cow pasture at Cambe, with all the lands of Wilden, Scakilden and Erghum, and at Hood they were allowed to erect a timber church and house. The community resided there for four years, and then, finding the place unsuitable, they removed to Old Byland, where they built a small cell on the banks of the Rye, assisted once again by the compassionate Roger de Mowbray.

The site of the former fortress at Thirsk is in a public area known as Castle Garth just a short walk away from the bustling marketplace in the direction of the racecourse. The area that is grassed over to this day has never been built on, having served as a garden and paddock over the years. Adopted by Thirsk Town Council as an open space for the enjoyment of the community, it still bears traces of the original earthworks, namely the western bailey rampart and ditch. Part of the overgrown motte can still be seen in the garden to the left of a large Victorian villa. Much of the damage to the site had already been done well before I'Anson's time. 'The motte, which appears to have been a small one – probably merely used as a citadel – has been lowered and partially levelled, and is now crowned by a house dignified by the name of "Castle Villa." The ditches and ramparts of the oblong bailey, still known as "Castle Garth," may be traced in part, but are much mutilated.' Considered by I'Anson a former burgus fortress, like Skelton and Whorlton, the defences are thought to have extended eastwards as far as Kirkgate and the present marketplace. It has also been suggested that the site dates from before the Conquest and that the Normans simply built on existing earthworks, or added to them. Following the dismantling of the castle, the Mowbrays continued residing in Thirsk at their manor house, Woodhill (formerly la Wodehall), less than a mile north of the Church of St Mary's in Kirkgate.

THORNE

Sometimes referred to as 'Little Holland' due to the flat landscape that characterises the area, the ancient market town of Thorne lies roughly 10 miles northeast of Doncaster and dates back to the eighth century. In 633 a battle was fought on the heath near here between the Saxon forces of King Edwin of Deira and the combined forces of King Penda of Mercia and Cadwallon. On a site immediately north of the twelfth-century parish Church of St Nicholas, which stands in the centre of the town, are the remains of a motte and bailey castle built soon after the Conquest by the de Warenne family, earls of Surrey. Known as Peel Hill, the site might have been used as a hunting lodge connected with Hatfield Chase and is one of a group of such castles commanding the Don valley. The well-preserved motte and a partial ditch that would originally have surrounded the motte still exist, but other features, such as ramparts and a bailey, are obscured by modern, urban developments. References to the castle in seventeenth-century texts indicate that the entrance was in Stonegate not far from the church, suggesting that the bailey was to the south.

Writing in 1534, Leland confirmed that a motte tower still existed in the sixteenth century and was used as a jail. But Casson, writing in 1829, said that this had been demolished and that only the foundations survived. These were found to be between 4 and 5ft thick and comprised rounded stones and cement. Sixty years earlier the motte had been deepened on the western side for use as a fishpond and a large part of the motte had collapsed into it. Casson further noted that the owner, a market gardener, had demolished part of the foundations and lowered the motte considerably. A few iron arrowheads, brass coins and a fragment of stained glass were found at that time, and subsequent excavations hinted at the motte having had a round keep, similar but smaller than that at Conisbrough where the de Warennes also held the manor. Citing a Dr Miller, Casson wrote that it was not improbable that materials from the castle had been used in constructing the Old Hall, which was built of stone and brick in 1575.

TICKHILL

Located 7 miles south of Doncaster, the historic town of Tickhill is home to one of Yorkshire's most southerly fortresses. Tickhill, or Dadesley as it was previously known, was already a large and wealthy Saxon settlement before 1066 when Earl Edwin of Mercia owned much of the land. After the Conquest William the Conqueror gave many of Edwin's manors to Roger de Busli, Earl of Shrewsbury, who at some point before 1089 built a motte and bailey castle. Originally referred to as Blyth Castle due to the relative obscurity of Dadesley, Roger also founded a priory here in 1088. Like other imposing castles such as those at Helmsley, Middleham, Pickering, Scarborough and Skipton, the earthworks at Tickhill are a prominent feature of the town. Located just south of the town centre, the castle was later reinforced in masonry, possibly by Roger himself before his death in 1098, or in 1102 when a curtain wall was built following a siege. Whatever the truth, the reinforcement of the fortress at Tickhill proved a wise decision considering the castle was at the centre of conflict for centuries.

Roger died without issue and the castle fell into the hands of the powerful Robert de Belesme. He backed the wrong side in an attempt to usurp the English throne, which infuriated Henry I and resulted in the previously mentioned siege of 1102. The garrison eventually surrendered and Robert fled abroad, only to be captured in 1112 and imprisoned for life. In the meantime, the fortress at Tickhill was now in the hands of the Crown, where it remained until 1139. In that year Stephen gave it to John, Count of Eu, who was a de Busli descendant. John was captured in 1141 at the Battle of Lincoln and a decade later the manor had a new lord in Ranulph de Gernon, 4th Earl of Chester. Ranulph's tenure was short-lived because he was murdered by poisoning two years later and the castle reverted once more to the Crown.

In 1178 a major undertaking by Henry II saw the building of a massive stone keep on top of the motte. The walls were 3m thick and the keep was not completed until after his death in 1189. His son Richard I succeeded to the throne, but when he left England for the Third Crusade in 1190, his brother Prince John lost no time in taking control of Tickhill Castle. It was only following a siege after Richard's return in 1194 that the castle was surrendered. However, Richard died in 1199 and John became king. The castle remained in royal hands until 1362, when it was given to John of Gaunt, Duke of Lancaster. Over the next two centuries it descended into ruin and it was only in 1614 that its lease to the Hanby family saved it from further decay. During the English Civil War, the castle was refortified as a Royalist stronghold, but in 1644 it was surrendered to the Parliamentarians who slighted its defences and demolished the keep built by Henry II.

The house and grounds were extensively remodelled in the eighteenth century and the Duchy of Lancaster still owns the castle up to the present day. Currently on lease, public access is limited to just one half-day per year. Sadly there is no external vantage point from which visitors can obtain a good view.

TOPCLIFFE

Situated in the Vale of York between Thirsk and Ripon, Topcliffe is a quiet village on the River Swale that became synonymous with the famed 'Darrowby' in the popular James Herriot books. The castle, known locally as Maiden Bower, was built in or about 1071 and is one of the most typical of Yorkshire's Norman earth and timber castles. It is especially important historically as it was the original English home of the great feudal house of Percy. We learn from Dugdale that founder William de Percy came to England in 1067 from Perci in the department of La Manche and joined the king during his expedition to Scotland in 1072. On his return from this campaign, he co-supervised the rebuilding of York Castle and was subsequently appointed governor of the city of York. He was also the chief Yorkshire feudatory of his friend Hugh d'Avranches, Earl of Chester. Despite their wealth and power, the lot of the Percy family was not a happy one. 'The history of the Percy family is a scene of war and blood,' wrote Whellan in 1857. 'Six of the earls died violent deaths, as did many of the collateral branches.'

The castle site commands excellent views over the surrounding countryside and was impressive even in I'Anson's day: 'The well-preserved and interesting motte and bailey castle occupies the nab end

The castle site at Topcliffe is located on private ground behind Manor Farmhouse and the farmer's permission is required to view.

of a low, natural ridge rising above low-lying and somewhat swampy ground between the River Swale on the south and the Cod Beck on the north, which streams effect a junction a short distance to the east of the fortress. There can be no doubt whatever that the land between the two streams and around the ridge on which the fortress stood was a swamp, and that the castle thus occupied a highly defensible position on what would then be practically an island. The motte rises some 45 feet above the low-lying ground between the two streams, viewed from which it is very formidable in appearance.' In 1174, when the castle was garrisoned for King Henry II during the de Mowbray rebellion, the timber defences were strengthened (Pipe Rolls).

There is no record of when the castle fell into disuse, but I'Anson summised that Topcliffe 'was probably the principal residence of the Percy family until the acquisition by purchase, early in the fourteenth century, of the Vesci castle of Alnwick, yet it never developed any works in masonry and is one of several examples of an early Norman

A view looking south over Cod Beck showing the full extent of the bailey at Topcliffe.

timber castle being occupied by an important baronial family down to a comparatively late date'. The subsequent building of the huge moated manor house showed the significance of Topcliffe to the Percy family. 'There is no doubt that this manor house was of considerable size,' wrote I'Anson. Allegedly the manor house was also the scene of more spilled Percy blood. 'It has been stated that the [4th] Earl of Northumberland was murdered here on April 28, 1489, by an infuriated mob,' continued I'Anson. 'That grasping and insatiable person, Henry VII, had ordered the Earl to levy an unpopular tax, which the Yorkshire people, by whom his predecessor, Richard III, had been greatly beloved, much resented. When the Earl was compelled to admit to the assembled people that the royal miser intended to enforce payment of the tax, they suddenly attacked and slew him.' The earl was carried from Topcliffe to Beverley in an enormous procession, spending the night at the Percy manor houses in Wressle and Leconfield. He was interred in the Percy Chantry of Beverley Minster, where his magnificent altar tomb can still be seen.

Despite being free of encroachment by modern developments (although the bulldozers that created the runway of the nearby airfield for RAF Bomber Command in 1940 almost did untold damage), some disfigurement was inevitable. 'Unfortunately the motte has been somewhat mutilated by three very narrow terraces or steps being cut in its sides, this doubtlessly being done when the earthworks were included as an ornament in the grounds of the later manor-house of the Percy family to the immediate west of the Norman fortress,' wrote I'Anson. Even without this mutilation, which reduced the diameter of the summit of the motte, I'Anson still considered the space within the stockaded enclosure insufficient to allow the erection of a detached tower. 'It seems probable that the stockade would bear one or more small timber turrets on its enceinte in order to provide a certain amount of accommodation in the citadel.' The motte is separated from the

The earthworks to the immediate right of the bridge mark the site of the later manor house of the Percy family.

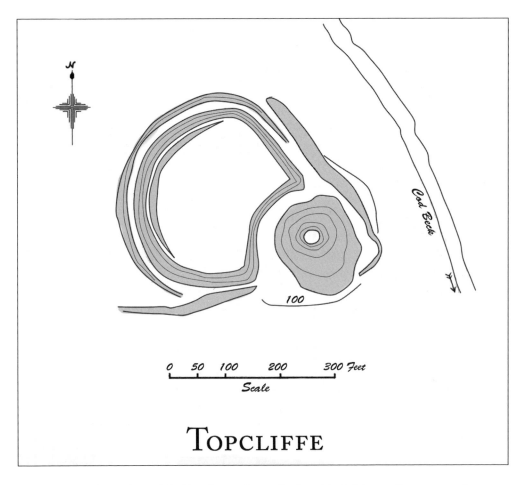

N

Cod Beck

100

0   50   100   200   300 Feet

Scale

Topcliffe

horseshoe-shaped bailey by a deep ditch with fairly well-preserved banks. As there is no gap in the bailey ramparts, I'Anson suggested that the entrance must have been via a light flying bridge of timber, which could be let down or drawn up as needed. The Bayeux Tapestry has an example of horses being trained to climb up this kind of bridge. I'Anson further suggested that the timber great hall would probably have been placed at the south side of the bailey with windows facing south towards the River Swale.

WAKEFIELD
The city of Wakefield (Wachfeld in the Domesday Book) grew from just a small settlement here in the fifth or sixth century, probably due to the old Roman road between Pontefract and Manchester, which

crossed the River Calder via a ford near the site of Wakefield Bridge. After the Conquest the manor was granted by William I to William de Warenne, 1st Earl of Surrey, whose descendant William, 3rd Earl of Surrey probably built the motte and bailey castle on a site known as Lowe Hill. Located in Thornes Park on a hilltop overlooking the River Calder, it offers extensive views across the city that eventually grew around it. Little is known about the early history of the site, but excavations in 1953 support a date of construction in the mid-twelfth century, which coincides with the war between Stephen and Matilda (1138–1149). The nearest early Norman fortress (Sandal), which is barely a mile to the southeast on the opposite side of the River Calder, was first mentioned in an ancient text of the same period and it is possible that they were built contemporaneously to control river traffic.

Writing in 1879–1880, Clark was in no doubt that the motte at Lowe Hill is artificial, but was equally certain that it already existed at the time of the Norman Conquest. 'There can be no question that Lowe or Law Hill is a Burh similar to those recorded in the Anglo-Saxon Chronicle as thrown up by Eadward the Elder (901–925) and Aethelflaeda (911–918).' Similarly its occupation by the Normans in conjunction with the fortress at Sandal seemed obvious to Clark. 'The two works are a short mile apart, and may have been intended, like those at York, Stamford, Hertford and Buckingham, to defend passage up the stream.'

A century after it was built the castle was abandoned and by the time of Leland's *Itinerary* (1535–1543) there existed a tradition that it was destroyed by natural causes, possibly a great storm. 'A quarter of a mile withowt Wakefeld apperith an hille of erth caste up, wher sum say that one of Erles Warines began to build and as fast as he buildid violence of winde defacid the work. This is like a fable. Sum say that it was nothing but a wind mille hill. The place is now caullid Lohille. The toune of Wakefeld streachith out al in lenght by est and west, and hath a fair area for a market place. The building of the towne is meately faire, most of tymbre, but sum of stone.' There is no evidence to suggest that the castle ever developed works in masonry. However, had it been reinforced in stone at some later date, it would have served as a handy quarry for an expanding Wakefield.

WHITWOOD

Officially part of Wakefield, the small community of Whitwood lies on the southern bank of the River Calder where the unscheduled remains of a motte and bailey castle are on the fringe of a golf course, close to an industrial site. Known variously as Ferry Hill, Fairies Hill and Castle Hill, the site might have been chosen to command an important river crossing, as the name Ferry Hill suggests. Despite rivers being fuller and more extensively used for traffic in medieval times, a motte found close to a waterway that is not navigable probably means it existed to extract a toll from road travellers. And Whitwood stands at a spot where the direct road from Pontefract to Leeds would cross the Calder (Armitage, 1912).

The extensive manor of Wakefield belonged to the earls of Warenne from about 1090 to 1347 and the family built earth and timber castles at Lowe Hill and Sandal. The former was abandoned when Sandal became the caput of the manor. Various names are associated with having held Whitwood as subfeudaries of the Warennes, including Roger Peitevin and Robert de Lacy. So who actually built the fortress is uncertain. However, despite doubt that the motte was man-made and not simply waste dumped from Whitworth Colliery, excavations in 2006 showed it to be of layered construction without the usual signs of industrial waste. On top of this, faint traces of a ditch also survive. Moreover, Leland's *Itinerary* (1535–1543) actually mentions a castle being located here: 'There I saw in an enclosid pasture ground the hilles of an old castelle hard upon the ripe of Calder river. It is now caullid Castel Hille and belongith to one Archibald Giseland of Lincolnshire.' A twelfth-century pottery find close to the site also suggests its authenticity as an early Norman site.

WHORLTON

The earthwork at Whorlton is romantically located on the western edge of the North York Moors escarpment and overlooks the village of Swainby. The castle enclosures would have formed a 'burgus' or village that included the original Holy Cross Church. I'Anson was enamoured: 'Standing at the western end of the large enclosure, [the castle] is very pleasantly situated at the entrance to Scugdale,

Whorlton Castle viewed from the direction of Whorl Hill to the east.

immediately to the west of Whorl Hill, on a spur which projects westward towards the low-lying country. It commands extensive views to the north and west, is admirably placed for defensive purposes, and is not far distant from a branch Roman road leading to Yarm.'

I'Anson was convinced that the motte was originally higher than it is today, but was lowered during the reign of Richard II when the tower and gatehouse were built in stone. 'There is no doubt that it [the motte] was of sufficient size to have borne a timber tower of the first magnitude and may have been crowned by a great wooden keep containing both great hall and private apartments, in other words that the tower may have been a "palace keep" such as we get in stone at Middleham. The bailey probably merely contained the stabling, outhouses, etc., and there are no indications that it ever developed masonry, the stone castle being confined to the summit of the lowered motte.'

The view from Whorlton Castle looking northeast towards Whorl Hill and with Roseberry Topping in the far distance.

Whorlton commands extensive views to the northwest.

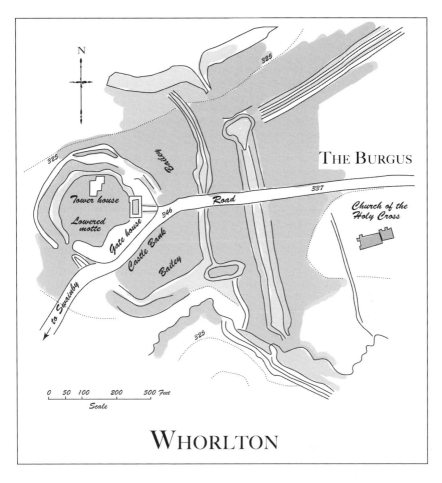

Figures on map: N, 325, 325, 337, 346, 325, 325

Tower house
Lowered motte
Gate house
Castle Bank
Bailey
Bailey
Road
to Swainby
THE BURGUS
Church of the
Holy Cross

0   50 100   200   500 Feet
Scale

WHORLTON

After the Norman Conquest, the Whorlton estate belonged to Robert, Earl of Mortain and of Cornwall. Nigel Fossard acquired it after the Mortain rebellion of 1088 and early in the reign of Henry I (1100–1135) it passed by marriage to Robert de Meynell to whom the castle is attributed. Works in masonry might not have developed until after 1200, according to I'Anson. 'At the time of the accession of Henry II [1154] there is no doubt that Whorlton was an earth and timber castle of the usual Norman type; but it may have developed works in masonry during the lifetime of Robert de Meynell II, c.1200, and is mentioned in 1216 as the castle of Potto.' Whatever the case, by 1343 the castle was described as 'ruinous'.

Alternatively known as 'Hwernelton' Castle, Whorlton remained in the possession of the de Meynell family, creators of Whorlton Park,

129

until passing successively into the hands of Robert de Roos and Hugh de Balliol. It was eventually restored to the family again, but when Nicholas de Meynell died without a male heir in 1342, his lands passed to the Archbishop of Canterbury. In 1348 it was partially restored to the de Meynell family through the female line with the remainder going to the Crown. It subsequently passed by marriage to the Darcy family and then once again by marriage to the Strangways family, in whose possession it remained until 1541. Following rival family claims to the estate, it came into the ownership of the Crown until passing to the Earl of Lennox in 1544 and to Lord Kinloss in 1603, from whose family it was privately bought in the late nineteenth century.

The castle site is fenced off and on private land, but can be viewed from the road between Swainby and Whorlton. The Black Horse in Swainby is a convenient watering hole for weary travellers.

YAFFORTH

Little is known about the earthwork at Yafforth, which is a quiet village on the River Wiske about 1 mile west of Northallerton. It is thought that the motte castle situated immediately northwest of the village and known locally as Howe Hill was erected by Alan Niger during the

Howe Hill at Yafforth once commanded a ford on the River Wiske.

130

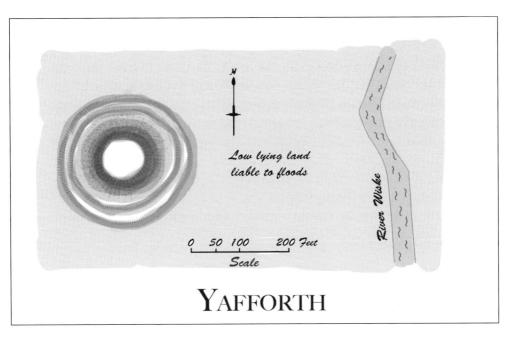

YAFFORTH

reign of Stephen (1135–1154). The site commanded a ford on the Wiske and the swamp surrounding it would have formed an excellent natural defence, as I'Anson found out when he visited it more than 100 years ago. 'On the occasion of three visits by the writer to the site of this castle, in the middle of the summer of 1912, all the fields around it were under water – owing to the long-continued wet weather – and he was informed by the tenant farmer that his hay, then floating about in some six inches of water had been cut some weeks previously, but that he had never had an opportunity of getting it into cock.' Despite the state of the surrounding land, I'Anson hinted at where the entrance to the stronghold had been and estimated that the degree of shelter and protection would have been very basic. 'There are faint indications that the entrance to the motte was on the north side, towards the west . . . . The accommodation afforded by this timber castle would probably be rude and primitive in the extreme, possibly consisting of a shed within the timber palisade.'

What we do know about Yafforth is that William de Brettevill (Bretevile) was granted the manor in 1197–1198 by Robert de la Mare. A century later, Baldwin de Brettevill held it and in 1316, William de Brettevill and Richard de Danby were returned as joint lords. In 1358–1360, Edward III granted custody of all lands and tenements in

Yafforth to John de Brettevill. But due to the death of a rightful male heir at Bosworth Field, the estate was divided and passed by marriage into various families. Notable gentry to have held estates in Yafforth include the Hawksworths, who held land in Little Danby and Yafforth until the Civil War; the Lascelles and Middleton families; the Meynells of Kilvington; Sir William Belasyse; Thomas, Lord Fauconberg; the Darcy family; Sir William Dalton of Hauxwell; and by marriage, Viscount Preston (Page, 1914).

The site is easily visible from the road leading between Yafforth and Danby Wiske.

YORK

York once boasted two castles, both built by William the Conqueror: the original York Castle built in 1068, which underlies the thirteenth-century Clifford's Tower, and a second fortress at Baile Hill on the opposite (west) bank of the River Ouse. Both fortresses were of earth and timber construction and although it is generally held that the latter was built a year later, there is a theory suggesting that William actually

Now just a tree-grown mound, Baile Hill in York was once the site of an earth and timber fortress built by William the Conqueror.

Baile Hill viewed from the west – looking towards the River Ouse.

built the Baile Hill fortress before crossing over to the east bank of the Ouse to build York Castle (Cooper, 1904). The chronicle of Orderic Vitalis (1075–1142) states that one castle was built in 1068 and the other when William returned to York at the beginning of 1069 (Armitage, 1912). Whatever the truth, the casual visitor to York can be forgiven for not realising that a castle once existed on the west bank of the Ouse. The Baile Hill earthwork (baile meaning an enclosure or courtyard in Norman French) is located at the junction of Baile Hill Terrace and Cromwell Road and the popular belief is that William built the castle there following a rebellion the year after seizing York. Both castles were of the motte and bailey type and were destroyed in September 1069 by English and Danish armies. However, they were quickly rebuilt and by Christmas of that same year William held a triumphant feast in York (*Anglo-Saxon Chronicle*). The fortress on the west bank became known as the 'Old Baile' and its motte, which is all that remains visible today, is best viewed from the city wall immediately next to it.

The bailey at Old Baile originally lay to the northwest of the motte and was rectangular. It extended to almost 3 acres and had an earth rampart with an outer ditch. The main bailey at York Castle on the east

An impression of York's twin earth and timber castles when they were first built by the Conqueror.

Tell-tale dips in the city wall rampart hint at where ditches once existed.

bank lay to the southeast and extended down to the line of the River Foss. A large bailey also existed to the northeast. The present bailey of York Castle does not follow the lines of the original one, but is an enlargement made in 1825 (Armitage, 1912). The Old Baile is believed to have been in regular use for only a short period of time. Originally it stood well outside the city walls (Cooper, 1904). In the thirteenth century it became enclosed in the new stone walls that had been carried along the west and south banks of the Old Baile (Armitage, 1912). By this time it was in the hands of the Archbishop of York and in the early fourteenth century a dispute arose between the archbishop and the city fathers about who was responsible for defending the Old Baile in times of war. Between 1317 and 1340 the fortifications were strengthened, first using timber and then masonry. By 1487 the Old Baile was under the jurisdiction of the city's mayor and eventually became integrated into the city wall on the southeast and southwest sides. It was used as

This small engraving on the city-walls walkway commemorates the time when York had two mighty fortresses.

135

a gun emplacement during the English Civil War and before that the site served as a pasture for grazing animals. It was also used for recreational activities, such as archery. This continued right up to the nineteenth century. But the site suffered from urban expansion during the latter part of this period and in 1802 some of the land was used for the city's new house of correction. When that was demolished in 1882, it was replaced by housing, which remains to this day. At the time of Leland's *Itinerary* (1535–1543) the demarcation lines of the bailey were still clearly visible. There are, however, two slight dips in the city wall rampart that indicate where the former bailey ditch stood: one is next to Baile Hill and the other close to Victoria Bar.

Bibliography

Addy, S.O., *Some Defensive Earthworks In The Neighbourhood Of Sheffield* (1914)

Allcroft, A. Hadrian, *Earthwork of England* (London, 1908), pp. 406, 408

Armitage, Ella S., *A key to English antiquities with special reference to the Sheffield and Rotherham district* (J.M. Dent and Co., London, 1905)

Armitage, Ella, *The Early Norman Castles of the British Isles* (John Murray, London, 1912)

Armitage and Montgomerie, in Page, William (ed.), *VCH Yorkshire*, Vol. 2, 1912, p. 45

Armstrong, Leslie, *Sheffield Castle: An Account of Discoveries made during excavations on the site from 1927 to 1929. Transactions of the Hunter Archaeological Society IV*, 1930, *pp. 7–27*

Atkinson, J.C., *Forty Years in a Moorland Parish* (1891 reprint. MTD Rigg Publications, 1987)

Brooke, Sir Thomas, Bart, F.S.A., *Yorkshire Archaeological Journal* (1901)

Brown, R. Allen, 'A List of Castles, 1154–1216', *English Historical Review*, Vol. 74, 1959, p. 249–280 (repr. Brown, R. Allen, *Castles, conquest and charters: collected papers*, (Boydell Press, Woodbridge, 1989), pp. 90–121)

Brown, William (ed.), *Yorkshire inquisitions of the reigns of Henry III and Edward I*, Vol. 1 (Yorkshire Record Series 12, 1892), pp. 63–65

Buck, Samuel and Nathaniel, *Buck's Antiquities*, Vol. 2 (London, 1774), p. 336

Buckland, P. and Dolby, M., 'Doncaster', *Current Archaeology*, Vol. 33, 1972, pp. 273–277

Bulmer, *Topography, History and Directory (Private and Commercial) of North Yorkshire* (S&N Publishing, 1890), p. 723

Bulmer, *History and Directory of East Yorkshire* (1892)

Butler, Lawrence, 'The Origins of the Honour of Richmond and its Castles' (1994)

Camden, William, *Britannia* (1607)

Casson, W., *History and Antiquities of Thorne* (1829)

Chalkley Gould, I., 'Some early defensive earthworks of the Sheffield district', *Journal of the British Archaeological Association*, Vol. 10 (1904)

Chandler, John, *John Leland's Itinerary: travels in Tudor England*, (Sutton Publishing, 1993), p. 560

Château Gaillard, Vol. 16, pp. 69–80, (repr. in Liddiard, Robert (ed), *Anglo-Norman Castles*, (Boydell Press, Woodbridge, 2003), pp. 91–103)

Clark, G.T., 'Observations on some moated mounds in Yorkshire', *Yorkshire Archaeological Journal,* Vol. 6 (1879–80), pp. 109–112

Clark, G.T., *Medieval Military Architecture in England* (1884)

Clark, G.T., 'Contribution towards a complete list of moated mounds or burhs', *The Archaeological Journal*, Vol. 46 (1889)

Clarkson, Christopher, *The History of Richmond in the County of York* (Bowman, 1821), p. 312

Collingwood, R.G., *The Archaeology of Roman Britain*, (Methuen, 1930), pp. 104–106

Constable, Christopher, *Aspects of the archaeology of the castle in the north of England c. 1066-1216* (doctoral thesis, Durham University, 2003)

Cooper, Thomas Parsons, *York: The Story of its Walls, Bars and Castles*, (E. Stock, London, 1904)

Crabtree, John, *A concise history of the parish and vicarage of Halifax* (1836), p. 401

Crosfield, A., *The History of Northallerton in the County of York* (Langdale, York, 1791)

Dallaway, J., *A series of Discourse upon Architecture in England* (1833), p. 272

Davies, D., Wood, S., Clarke, G., *Pickhill North Yorkshire A Village History* (2000)

Dawson, W.H., *History of Skipton* (London, 1882), pp. 65–86

Delderfield, E.R., *Kings and Queens of England and Great Britain* (David & Charles, 1966)

Dennison, E., 'A Survey of Hood Hill Castle', *The Ryedale Historian*, No. 21 (2002–2004), pp. 26–29

Eastmead, W., *Historia Rievallensis* (1824), p. 87

English, B., *The Lords of Holderness 1086–1260 – A Study in Feudal Society* (Oxford University Press, 1979)

Farrer, William (ed.), *Early Yorkshire Charters*, Vol. 1 to 4 (1914–1916)

Fleming, Andrew, *Swaledale. Valley of the Wild River* (Edinburgh University Press, 1998)

Fowler, J.T. (ed.), 'Historia Selebiensis monasterii', in *The Coucher Book of Selby* (Yorkshire Archaeological Society Record Series 10), Vol. 1, 1891, pp. 33–39

Fox, G., *History of Pontefract in Yorkshire* (Pontefract, 1827)

Gould, I.C., 'Early Defensive Earthworks', *Journal of the British Archaeological Association*, Vol. 7 (1901)

Grainge, W., *The Castles and Abbeys of Yorkshire* (Whittaker & Co., London, 1855)

Grape, Wolfgang, *The Bayeux Tapestry – Monument to a Norman Triumph* (Prestel, 1994)

Graves, J., *History of Cleveland, in the North Riding of the County of York* (F. Jollie & Sons, Carlisle, 1808), p. 145

Grose, Francis, *Antiquities of England and Wales* (London, 1785, new edn. orig. 1756), Vols. 6 and 8

Hardy, T.D. (ed.), *Rotuli Chartarum, 1199–1216* (Record Commission, 1837), p. 44

Harvey, Alfred, *Castles and Walled Towns of England* (Methuen and Co., London, 1911)

Harwood Brierley, 'The village where Wordsworth was married', *Notes and Queries* (Series 8, 1896), Vol. 9, pp. 62–63

Hey, David, *Medieval South Yorkshire*, (Landmark Publishing, 2003)

Hey, David, *A History of Sheffield,* 3rd ed., (Carnegie Publishing Ltd, Lancaster, 2010)

Higham, Mary, 'The Mottes of North Lancashire, Lonsdale and South Cumbria', *Transactions of the Cumberland and Westmoreland Antiquarian and Archaeological Society*, Vol. 91 (1991), pp. 79–90

Hills, G.M., 'Examples of ancient earthworks', *Journal of the British Archaeological Association*, Vol. 30 (1874), pp. 406–413

Hunter, Joseph, 'Hallamshire. The History and Topography of the Parish of Sheffield in the County of York' (Lackington, Hughes, Harding, Mayor & Jones, London, 1819)

I'Anson, W.M., 'The castles of the North Riding', *The Yorkshire Archaeological Journal*, Vol. 22 (Yorkshire, 1913), pp. 303–399

I'Anson, W.M., 'The castles of the North Riding' *The Yorkshire Archaeological Journal*, Vol. 24 (Yorkshire, 1913), pp. 258–262

Illingworth, J.L., *Yorkshire's Ruined Castles*, (Wakefield, 1938, republished 1970)

Jessop, C.M., 'Observations respecting Aldborough', *Journal of the British Archaeological Association*, Vol. 5 (1850), pp. 74–75

Jones, John, *The History and Antiquities of Harewood* (Simpkin Marshall and Co., London, 1859), pp. 32, 248–9

Journal of Sedbergh and District History Society, Vol. 4, No. 1, (1998)

Kent, G.H.R., 'Middle division: Swine', *VCH Yorkshire: East Riding*, Vol. 7 (2002)

King, D.J.C., *Castellarium Anglicanum* (Kraus, London, 1983), Vol. 2, p. 512

King, E., *Munimenta antiqua or Observations on antient castles* (W. Bulmer and Co., 1804), Vol. 3, pp. 43–72, 209

Lawson-Tancred, M.E., *A guide book to the antiquities of Aldborough and Boroughbridge and a short account of their history,* 3rd ed. (J. Topham & Son, Boroughbridge, 1948), p. 18

Mackenzie, J.D., *Castles of England; their story and structure*, (Macmillan, New York, 1896), Vol. 2

Magilton, J., *The Doncaster District* (1977)

Maxwell Lyte, H.C. (ed.), *Calendar of Patent Rolls Edward III (1327–30)*, Vol. 1 (1891), p. 31

Maxwell Lyte, H.C. (ed)., *Calendar of Patent Rolls Edward III (1350–54)*, Vol. 9 (1907), p. 218

Moorhouse, S.A., article in *Yorkshire Archaeological Journal*, Vol. 42 (1968)

Ord, J.W., *The History and Antiquities of Cleveland* (1846), p. 338

Page, William, *Victoria County History Yorkshire: North Riding Vol. 1* (1914)

Page, William, *Victoria County History Yorkshire: North Riding Vol. 2* (1923)

Pettifer, A., *English Castles, A guide by counties* (Boydell Press, Woodbridge, 1995), p. 310

Pipe Roll, 1205 (Public Record Office), *The Great Roll of the Pipe for the seventh year of the reign of King John Michaelmas 1205* (Pipe Roll Society 57)

Poulson, George, *The history and antiquities of the seigniory of Holderness, in the East-Riding of the county of York* (Thomas Topping Bowlalley Lane, Hull and W. Pickering, London, 1840)

Pipe Rolls, 1130–1200 (Public Record Office), *The Great Roll of the Pipe for . . .* [5–34 Henry II] (Pipe Roll Society, London, 1884–1925)

Raine, J., 'De Builli, the First Norman Lord of the Honour of Tickhill, and Founder of the Monastery of Blyth', *The History and Antiquities of the Parish of Blyth* (J.B. Nichols and Sons, Westminster, 1860)

Raine, J., *The historians of the church of York and its archbishops* (London, 1879), Vol. 1, p. 302

Renn, D.F., *Norman Castles of Britain*, 2nd ed. (John Baker, London, 1973), p. 88

Ryder, P.F., 'Ravensworth Castle, North Yorkshire', *Yorkshire Archaeological Journal*, Vol. 51 (1979), pp. 81–100

Ryder, P.F., *Medieval Buildings of Yorkshire* (Ash Grove Books, 1982)

Salter, Mike, *The Castles and Tower Houses of Yorkshire* (Folly Publications, Malvern, 2001), p. 16

Sheppard, Thomas, *The Lost Towns of the Yorkshire Coast* (A. Brown & Sons, London, 1912), p. 190

Smith, A.H., *The Place-names of the West Riding of Yorkshire 5* (Cambridge University Press, 1961), p. 80

Speight, H., *Romantic Richmondshire* (1897), pp. 189–190

Speight, Harry, *Lower Wharfedale* (E. Stock, London, 1902), pp. 214–215, 451–452

Stacye, J., 'Laughton en-le-Morthen (or Morthing)', *Journal of the British Archaeological Association*, Vol. 30 (1874)

Stephens, Tony and Gregory, Susan, 'Burton in Lonsdale in the late medieval period', *North Craven Heritage Trust Journal (manorial history)* (2006)

Teeside Archaeology, *Archaeological Booklet*, No. 5 (2012)

Thompson, A. Hamilton, *Military architecture in England during the Middle Ages* (Oxford University Press, 1912), pp. 166–171

Thompson W., 'Sedbergh, Garsdale and Dent' (Richard Jackson, Leeds, 1892) pp. 44–46

Timbs, J. and Gunn, A., *Abbeys, Castles and Ancient Halls of England and Wales, Vol. 3* (London, 1872)

Toulmin-Smith, Lucy (ed.), *The itinerary of John Leland in or about the years 1535–1543* (Bell and Sons, London, 1907), Vol. 1, pp. 41–42, 47; Vol. 2, p. 6; and Vol. 4, p. 27

Turner, Maurice, *Yorkshire Castles: Exploring Historic Yorkshire* (Westbury Publishing, Otley, 2004), pp. 92, 102, 109–110, 174, 234

Turner, T.H. and Parker, J.H., *Some account of Domestic Architecture in England* (Oxford, 1859), Vol. 3, Part 2

Nicholas Vincent, Thwing, Sir Robert (III), *Oxford Dictionary of National Biography* (Oxford University Press, 2004)

The Victoria History of the County of Yorkshire: Volume II, (1912)

Wainwright, *Strafford and Tickhill* (Sheffield, 1826)

Walker, J.W., 'Sandal Castle', *Yorkshire Archaeological Journal*, Vol. 13 (1895), pp. 154–188

Watson, J., *The History and Antiquities of The Parish of Halifax, in Yorkshire* (T. Lowndes, London, 1775), pp. 117–119

Whellan, T., *History and topography of the city of York and the North Riding of Yorkshire* (T. Whellan and Co., 1857)

Whitaker, A.H., 'Hood Castle', *Rydale Historian*, Vol. 5 (1970), pp. 36–40

Whitaker, T.D., *The History and Antiquities of the Deanery of Craven in the County of York* (London, 1812), pp. 322–51

Whitaker, T.D., *A History of Richmondshire in the North Riding of the County of York* (London, 1823), Vol. 2

Whitaker, T.D., (3rd edn edited by A.W. Morant), *The History and Antiquities of the Deanery of Craven in the County of York* (Leeds and London, 1878), pp. 395–420

White, H.M., 'Excavations in Castle Hill, Burton in Lonsdale', *The Antiquary*, Vol. 41 (1905), pp. 411–417

White, Robert, *The Yorkshire Dales. A Landscape Through Time* (Great Northern Books, 2002)

White, Robert, 'Introduction', in White, R.F. and Wilson, P.R. (eds), *Archaeology and Historic Landscapes of the Yorkshire Dales* (Yorkshire Archaeological Society, 2004), Occasional Paper No. 2, pp. 1–14

Yorkshire Archaeological Journal, Vol. 40, 1959, p. 5

Yorkshire Life, September 2013, p. 70–71

Young, George, *A history of Whitby, and Streoneshalh abbey; with a statistical survey of the vicinity to the distance of twenty-five miles*, Vol. 2, 1817, pp. 718–722 and 732–736

Index